The Politics of Crazy: How America Lost Its Mind and What We Can Do About It

By Chris Ladd

Edited by Karen Ostergren
Original art by Elisa Glass

Copyright © 2015 Chris Ladd

D0873768

Contents

Introduction

Americans have a well-earned reputation as friendly, hard-working, competent people. So why is the government they elect to represent them so frighteningly insane?

There is no point in resorting to euphemisms or hedged language. American politics in our age is an embarrassing circus. Looking back across our history, we find plenty of highs and lows, but there may have never been a period more deeply marked by batty, delusional politics.

We are not so much divided as dissociated. We are not merely debating the merits of different policies. We are arguing about the shape of reality.

The costs of our lengthening foray into political comedy are mounting. The last decade produced paranoia, greed, and lunacy so severe, it resulted in thousands of military and civilian casualties, compromised our national credibility, and eventually brought the global economy to its knees. The painful consequences did little to inspire restraint. Our political climate has actually gotten worse in the years following the financial collapse.

Since 2010, the legislative branch of the U.S. government has been effectively closed. The country is now governed by the executive branch and the bureaucracy, doing their best to meet basic demands within the legal framework that existed before Congress checked out.

We cannot carry on this way. America remains mind-bogglingly rich, powerful, and safe, more so than we can generally grasp. Yet there is only so much self-inflicted damage we can hope to endure. As wealthy and powerful as we are, so much remains for us to achieve, for ourselves and for the world if we are willing to sober up. The condition of our politics is a national disgrace that simply must end.

What if we had a realistic vision of where we are, what we have achieved, and what lies ahead for us to accomplish? We need not all agree on policies and plans if we can at least reach some consensus about what we are experiencing. The barest sense of orientation, some basic understanding of the general shape of reality, might be enough to get our heads on straight and start building again.

Many of these ideas first appeared on a blog called GOPLifer, authored by a lifelong Republican, but these essays are not expressly partisan. This series of short pieces is meant to sketch out a context through which to understand a rapidly changing world.

We are living through a wrenching global transformation so massive and so unexpected that we are still struggling to wrap our heads around it. It has brought us a landscape of benefits and challenges more promising than anything humans have experienced before.

For all its hopeful opportunities, this new environment is dazzlingly complex, with dangers that previous generations never faced. Dealing with this new world starts by seeing it with clear eyes. Only then can we, as citizens, start to think about policies and plans that will help us seize its opportunities and tame its dragons.

Part 1—Welcome to a New World

We live on the other side of a divide some scholars have called "the end of history," referring to the death of the great human struggle of political ideals. No comprehensive ideology is competing with liberal democracy on a global scale.

Yes, there are terrorists blowing up school buses and airplanes, but there are also bank robbers and serial killers, vandals and car thieves. None of them have a meaningful, globally persuasive ideology to offer. No matter what weapons they obtain or explosions they engineer, they cannot compete with us politically. They are at worst a massive, global criminal gang.

In short, we won.

We very suddenly find ourselves in a world that has been radically remade in ways we never anticipated. Global capitalism has made our lives dizzyingly fast and ruthlessly competitive. Rewards for those who were well positioned, high-performing, or just lucky have been stellar. The impact to those who were unprepared or vulnerable has been disappointing. Middle-class workers in the U.S. who faithfully followed the old rules have seen their world rocked and their fortunes severely dimmed. Life on Earth is better for the death of communism, but that great victory has delivered some surprises in its wake.

We got what we asked for, but we weren't ready to adapt to the demands of this new world. Progress means graduating to ever better and more-difficult problems, but politically we are clinging to the problems of the past. The challenges this new world has presented to us lay largely unnoticed and almost entirely unaddressed, sending an unpleasant but unidentified odor hovering over our victory like a dead varmint trapped in the walls.

Do you remember the scene at the end of the movie *Return of the Jedi*? (Stay with me here.)

The heroes are frolicking with those cuddly Ewoks, celebrating their final victory over the evil Empire. There are smiles and congratulations, singing and dancing. Then the film cuts to the credits.

Have you ever wondered which political coalitions controlled the new republic that emerged from the victory; which economic interests the new government would promote; how many Wookiees would have access to health care and at what cost?

No? Really?

You mean you haven't been waiting breathlessly all these years for *Star Wars Episode VII: Managing Currency Fluctuation for the Maximization of Galactic Trade Efficiencies?*

We live in the scenes that George Lucas never filmed, the ones that came after the victory. We are the heirs of the victory. Our battles, as brutal and complex as ever, are fought on a small scale against ambiguous enemies. There will be no liberator's triumph for us, just the policeman's satisfaction of a job well done—lives protected, and civilization maintained.

It is for us to build a new urban civilization in a world of scarce resources. To set rules for an economic order that has never before existed, rules that will preserve the dynamic wealth-creating power of global markets while taming the dangerous inequality that has followed in its wake. We must find ways to preserve individual liberty and human dignity in the face of the smothering power of a mostly benign central government.

So far, we are doing a monumentally lousy job of it. Like spoiled children handed the keys to the Porsche, we are in real danger of wrapping this fabulous machine around a light pole—while drunk and chock-full of antidepressants.

The challenges of our time require a different kind of steel. Whereas our ancestors battled charismatic villains, we're locked in a death struggle against our own diminished attention span. Our mission, regardless of whether we choose to accept it, is _administration_. Unfortunately, administration is boring.

Over the next decade or two, we will answer a set of questions that will determine how broadly the prosperity of this era is shared, how much of the world's population will get to participate, how many people will be killed by the instability that the new dynamism creates, and whether the U.S. will be a leader in this new era as by all rights it should be. We haven't begun to make plans to address these new questions, because they have emerged too quickly for us to recognize them.

The journey opens with the moment that best encapsulates the unique promise and danger of our time. Life, economics, and politics in a post-communist world have been defined by the lessons of 9/11—the other one.

The Other 9/11

On September 11, President George Bush gave one of the most insightful presidential addresses of our lifetimes. That speech might have been our historical turning point, the marker we crave that says, "Before this moment the world worked one way, and afterward things were different." However, hardly anyone remembers his speech because it didn't happen on _that_ September 11th and it wasn't delivered by _that_ George Bush.

In 1990, as the nation braced for the campaign to remove Iraqi forces from Kuwait, George H. W. Bush described the remarkable global transformation we were experiencing.

"We stand today at a unique and extraordinary moment ... A hundred generations have searched for this elusive path to

9

peace, while a thousand wars raged across the span of human endeavor. Today that new world is struggling to be born, a world quite different from the one we've known. A world where the rule of law supplants the rule of the jungle. A world in which nations recognize the shared responsibility for freedom and justice. A world where the strong respect the rights of the weak ... How we manage this crisis today could shape the future for generations to come."

From his vantage point on the edge of such a frightening conflict, President Bush recognized that the dynamics of global politics had changed. His speech was the bookend to an address given 50 years before, as Britain stood alone against the Nazis. Winston Churchill, in that dark moment, delivered a warning coupled with a promise:

"Hitler knows that he will have to break us in this island or lose the war. If we can stand up to him, all Europe may be freed and the life of the world may move forward into broad, sunlit uplands. But if we fail, then the whole world, including the United States, including all that we have known and cared for, will sink into the abyss of a new dark age ..."

Fifty years later, President Bush's speech on September 11, 1990, signaled our arrival on Churchill's "sunlit uplands." At long last, after so much blood sacrifice, we were standing on that promised ground, heirs to a world marked by rising freedom, prosperity, and rule of law that so many had dreamed of building.

Bush's speech could have inspired us to rub our eyes and look around, recognizing the beautiful new opportunities and fresh problems that surrounded us. We could have seized the chance to emerge from our Cold War defensive crouch, embracing a new, postwar order at home that would bring the freedom and prosperity of this new world to more people than ever before.

That is not what happened.

Faced with the relief of victory, we seem to be overcome by the toll of decades of trauma. Instead of seizing our new opportunities, we are breaking down into collective hysterics. On the "broad, sunlit uplands" promised to us, we are building bunkers stuffed with preserved food, ammo, and gold coins.

why are we scared

Yet the fact remains that we won the long, bloody wars of the 20th century. Despite the lost opportunities of the past few years, the world at large is vastly freer, wealthier, and friendlier to markets than it has ever been. The next American Century lies in pieces on our collective garage floor, waiting to be assembled.

The battle between Marxism and capitalism is over. Our challenge is preserving the relevance of public life in an environment far too dynamic for 20th-century "big government" to survive. Questions with no certain answers surround us. Ideological rigidity cannot guide us through these problems. We need a practical willingness to face facts and adapt solutions around our values.

It is time to move beyond 20th-century war logic and reckon with the challenges of our own time. We have to decide which September 11th will define our future.

Where the Crazy May Be Coming From

"Any sufficiently advanced technology is indistinguishable from magic." —Arthur C. Clarke

Our politics is getting weird. We've always struggled against opportunism and corruption and lying, but the fresh rise of what can be fairly described only as crazy is hitting us like an invasive species dropped into the local pond. The new creatures are crowding out the parasites we've learned to tolerate and eating everything in sight.

While there have always been some odd characters attracted to power, we seem to be dealing with a whole new category of crazy. GOP presidential polls in the 2012 nominating race were, at different times, led by: a billionaire and perennial pseudo-candidate with a terrible toupee whose rise was tied to the "birther" movement; a congresswoman who once accused the president of trying to set up mandatory, communist-style reeducation camps for youth; a Republican governor who claimed that Turkey, our NATO ally, is governed by "terrorists"; a former pizza company CEO and talk-show host with no political credentials who dismissed his complete ignorance of foreign-policy basics by complaining about the press. (His quote on the matter is too tasty not to repeat: "When they ask me who is the president of Ubeki-beki-beki-beki-stan-stan I'm going to say, 'You know, I don't know. Do you know?'"); and, of course, Ron Paul.

In 2013, Senator Ted Cruz rose to fame as a Senate rookie by insinuating that former Senator Chuck Hagel, a fellow Republican and then the nominee for Secretary of Defense, had been working for North Korea. He went on to earn further accolades for an effort to force the government to default on the national debt.

Senator James Inhofe of Oklahoma devoted an entire book to his claim that global warming is a hoax, a belief that has become pervasive among Republicans. Prominent Senator and likely 2016 Republican presidential candidate Rand Paul has stubbornly backed a Nevada rancher linked to white supremacists who refused to pay 20 years' worth of fees incurred by grazing on federal land, then assembled an armed mob to stop the government from collecting on his debts.

Congress has passed fewer laws since 2010 than at any other comparable period in modern history. Our government is deadlocked, incapable of addressing even mundane or routine national affairs.

Goofball theories backed by pure fantasy dominate mainstream political debate.

Rather than being hounded out of town, political figures who engage in absurd, inaccurate, and sometimes dangerous rhetoric become cult heroes. Facts are elitist. Credibility is evolving into a liability, and crazy has become a tactic.

There is a depressing irony at work inside this problem. Today, ordinary people have unprecedented access to reliable information, but falsehoods have proliferated alongside facts. It has never been easier to determine what's real, yet we seem more gullible than ever. This torrent of information, true and untrue, combined with an overwhelming pace of social change, may be undermining our ability to function. If so, what does that mean for representative government?

More than 40 years ago, Alvin Toeffler published *Future Shock*. In it he predicted that society had entered a phase of constant, wrenching, and ever-accelerating change. He expected this would lead to a form of social meltdown and a terrible strain on the individual mind. There's a comment from Toeffler's book that seems particularly prescient:

"And what then happens when an economy in search of a new purpose seriously begins to enter into the production of experiences for their own sake, experiences that blur the distinction between the vicarious and the non-vicarious, the simulated and the real? One of the definitions of sanity itself is the ability to tell real from unreal. Shall we need a new definition?"

Maybe we are in the process of redefining sanity on the public level. We have an abundance of reliable information to help us separate what is from what ain't, but we are also being overwhelmed by shiny distractions and unfiltered data. And it's not just omnipresent entertainment options that are weakening our hold on what's real. Reality itself is becoming perilously complex. Even the tools and devices that are most woven into the fabric of our daily lives are wonders beyond simple credibility. Consider this:

I have a device sitting on my desk that is barely larger than a credit card. It knows where I am on the globe at all times and can recommend a nearby restaurant I might like. It allows me to hold a conversation or exchange messages instantly with another person who may be thousands of miles away. It entertains me all day and night with music, games, movies, and news.

That statement is utterly, incredibly magical and at the same time absolutely real. And not a single human being on the planet—not one—understands all of the materials and technology required to create my smartphone sufficiently to build one by themselves, without assistance, from raw materials. Somewhere in the 20th century, our lives came to be dominated by technologies that were products of *cultures*, not *people*. We lost all individual control over them.

This world of credulous wonder and surplus information undermines politics, at least in the short run, by depriving us of what we most desire in evaluating public affairs: a singular narrative. In the old days, when there were three television stations, the dignified white men on the evening news gave us that calming gift. They had a staff of smart people who filtered the galaxy of world events for us and produced a storyline that we gobbled up at 5:30 p.m. Central.

With unfettered access to raw information we made a disturbing discovery: there is no single narrative, and there never was. What happens today is that 7 billion people experience 7 billion different things from 7 billion unique perspectives between every eyeblink. Most of them seem to be blogging about it.

The challenges of living in a world of rapidly accelerating change are not limited to technology. Growing cultural dynamism is touching chords of racial identity so deeply embedded that we barely understand them. For members of a generation that grew up with an unstated, yet also unchallenged, assumption of white supremacy, a faster, more integrated world is subjecting them to strange terrors.

Expanding access to better, more interesting food, music, movies and news is a wonderful development for most of us. Forty years ago, unless you lived in New York City your town almost certainly had no Thai restaurant. Unless you lived in the Rio Grande Valley or Southern California your grocery store probably did not sell tortillas. There were four, maybe five kinds of beer available, and none of them was more exotic than Lowenbrau. Not everyone is thrilled by these new choices. For some, the expansion of the unfamiliar signals a frightening decline in their cultural supremacy. In just a few decades many of their unstated and previously unconsidered assumptions about the world have crumbled, undermining their sense of security.

There were just as many homosexuals forty years ago as there are now, but almost all of them had the "decency" to hide, making it possible for everyone else to pretend that homosexuality was a choice pursued by deviants. Women were starting to participate in the workforce, but their new freedom to make economic and personal choices for themselves was still largely constrained by older cultural demands. The generation at the peak of its political power today grew up in a world that no longer exists.

Consider the life of former Texas governor and 2012 Republican presidential candidate Rick Perry. When he was a boy, white male workers faced no competition from African Americans, immigrants, women, or anyone else. The "n-word" was as ordinary as salt and pepper. The best jobs and housing were all set aside for white men. The best schools served them alone. White men mediated all access to the economy, the courts, church, education, medicine, and every other symbol of authority.

Women were finally allowed to enroll in Perry's beloved Texas A&M, the state's second-largest university system, on the basis of individually evaluated exceptions just two years before he started there. Throughout his college years, each female applicant had to receive the direct approval of the university's president. Women were not granted full admission rights at A&M until 1971.

Explicit racial segregation was illegal after 1964, but that barely dented the ingrained assumption of white male supremacy—at least at first. And though Jim Crow was largely a Southern phenomenon, the special status of white males was not. White men understood that God had made them racially supreme, the benevolent protectors of the weaker sex and even-weaker neighboring races. Law and culture made that supremacy feel like a reality until the federal government and global economic competition began to strip it away. The loss of that special status is feeding powerful anxiety in an older generation.

As change accelerates into a blur, our reality is refracting into a mosaic with no discernable pattern. Former moorings have suddenly collapsed. Stripped of religious and cultural assumptions that helped simplify our lives, we are left on our own to figure out what it all means, trying to translate our experiences into the coherent story that our increasingly outgunned monkey brains so desperately crave by using technology we can never hope to understand.

More and more we respond by shutting out the assault of cognitive dissonance and retreating from any unwelcome input. We carefully surround ourselves with news outlets, friends, and even neighbors who reinforce what we want to believe. We are building our own reality to support our chosen narrative, an exercise that is rotting our politics.

The retreat from dissonance leaves citizens locked in rhetorical bunkers, isolated from voices that might point out factual errors or logical flaws. Our political views have become self-reinforcing, regardless of errors or consequences. The feedback loop is broken.

Why do we so stubbornly cling to flawed political convictions in spite of the damage they create? Because the consequences of bad politics are felt collectively more than individually. Even when the consequences are severe, the chain of causation is often cloudy. That old problem has become worse in light of some changes brought about by the triumph of global capitalism.

Smart People, Stupid Politics

Perhaps at some point during 2013 you saw an email, Facebook post, or tweet from a seemingly reasonable friend containing a disturbing insight. It shared evidence suggesting that the Sandy Hook school shooting was staged by the government as a pretext to take away our guns.

Although the claim is completely nuts, it may have come from a perfectly sane adult, someone fully capable of making intelligent, responsible decisions in matters affecting his or her family or job. A startling number of people who make sound, well-reasoned decisions in their personal lives are comfortable engaging with political ideas that are empirically false and in some cases downright insane.

Conspiracy theories in politics are nothing new, but the degree to which they have entered mainstream political discourse is shocking and unprecedented—think Benghazi or the United Nations' Agenda 21. We seem to have no filters remaining to prevent ludicrous ideas from reaching the highest levels of policy. Sometime over the past decade or so, the politics of crazy jumped the tinfoil barrier and started to influence the political opinions of educated people who are otherwise competent and intelligent.

Although the politics of paranoia has become a Republican staple in the past few years, it is a mistake to imagine that this is a unique illness of our political right, or to blame it purely on the Internet. The "age of crazy" is a product of broad social forces that will soon affect Democrats as deeply as Republicans. Just search the Internet for the phrase _Monsanto Protection Act_ to see the Democratic version of loony politics. We cannot begin to formulate some response until we acknowledge the forces responsible for undermining our political sanity.

Political reason does not come from the same sources as individual reason. In our personal lives, we learn to shun stupid or ill-advised ideas, because we recognize or experience firsthand the damage they produce. We seldom apply the same rigor to politics that we bring to decisions affecting our work or families. The consequences of accepting poor advice in our personal lives can often be sharp, immediate, and expensive. The consequences of believing stupid political rumors are usually distant, deferred, and diluted among millions of people.

The personal gratification we derive from embracing ideas that reinforce our biases, no matter how patently stupid or damaging those ideas may be, is too powerful for many people to resist. There is comfort in our preconceptions. As the onslaught of information from around the globe undermines old ideas about the world, the urge to block out the cognitive dissonance, regardless of the collective cost, can be overwhelming.

Traditionally, we have accounted for the lack of individual feedback in politics by filtering public opinion in two ways. First, instead of direct democracy, we have a system of representative democracy in which we elect trustworthy citizens to decide political matters on our behalf. We hold these representatives accountable in the broad sweep, but defer to their judgment on the fine details.

Second, a dense network of social-capital institutions has always mediated our political environment, filtering out the dumb and the crazy while promoting into higher positions people who show promise in dealing with local matters. The stark, sudden decline of reason in our politics can perhaps be traced to the combined effects of a generation's worth of social and political changes that have left us more distant from public affairs, undermined our interest in responsible citizenship, and corroded this network.

In short, three factors account for the bulk of the crazy in our political system: The collapse of social-capital institutions in the face of a consumer culture, the increasing complexity of our world, and the struggle of one generation in particular to cope with the consequences of complexity, what Alvin Toeffler described as "future shock."

Not everyone is straining under the pressure of our constantly accelerating world. Many of those born in recent decades—the technology natives—seem largely untouched by future shock, even unable to comprehend it. As this new generation comes of age politically, some of the cultural impacts of the knowledge economy may take care of themselves.

The Post—Future Shock Generation

At Christmas a few years ago, we gave my son a Star Trek phaser and communicator. The toys were impressive replicas complete with all the features and details from the original series. He was initially very excited about them, but then an interesting thing happened.

Once all the wrapping was cleaned up and the Christmas high descended into the Christmas hangover, he disappeared with his new phone. It was nothing special, a flip-phone that came free with our family plan, but it was his constant companion. As near as I can tell, after Christmas dinner the phaser was never touched again. One of the finest technical accomplishments of the imaginary 23rd century paled in comparison to a 21st-century giveaway.

With a few exceptions, the gadgets imagined by the writers of Star Trek are embarrassingly inadequate in comparison to cheap consumer toys we now take for granted. In just four decades, we've outrun the farthest limits of the prior generations' technological imagination. Let's face it: Captain Kirk's communicator is a useless piece of crap. You can't tweet from it. It doesn't take pictures. It doesn't stream music or locate the nearest Chipotle.

The vision of the future described by Alvin Toeffler in *Future Shock* has proved remarkably accurate, but he failed to anticipate one important aspect of this transition. Future shock would, in a sense, end. It was an experience unique to those who still remembered an older, slower, more predictable world. While older Americans fall apart under the rising pressure of global competition, relentless anachronism, and disintegrating social norms, a younger generation shrugs. It's fine.

You can't miss what you never knew. Americans under 30 have no memory of permanence, stability, privacy, or boredom. They have grown into adulthood as knowledge-economy natives. The only shock they experience comes from power outages.

We may be experiencing a generation gap larger and more meaningful than the one that rocked our culture in the '60s. For the first time in decades, young people are maturing in a world that bears virtually no resemblance to their parents' experience. The gap is starkly visible in politics and religion.

The generation at the peak of its power and influence remains deeply marked by religious and political norms that are increasingly irrelevant to Americans under 30. Older voters on the left and right alike look more conservative than their younger counterparts.

Whereas older voters value tradition, younger voters crave authenticity. Politics for older voters is still dictated by race, conservative sexual and religious norms, and a suspicion of government—values that are largely meaningless to younger voters. Today's young are the most irreligious, post-racial, socially liberal generation we have ever raised.

Anyone who is expecting these kids to mellow and drift to the right as they age is kidding themselves. Contrary to popular myth, younger voters are not always more liberal than their elders and they do not necessarily get more conservative as they grow up. Reagan won massive majorities among the young. Voters under 30 remained a solid Republican block until the mid-'90s. Many of those Reagan-era youth, this writer included, have grown disenchanted with the GOP as the paranoid panic of the Future Shock generation has driven the party into a reactionary delirium. The young generation that embraced Reagan has drifted left as they aged.

Adapting to a world that renders science fiction quaint is a serious challenge for conservatives. Unfortunately, these are times that demand an intelligent, adaptive conservatism. Credible conservatism could prove to be a vital break, preserving crucial institutions and values that might otherwise be cast aside in the headlong chase for efficiency and money.

My kid still has those Star Trek toys. He rarely plays with them, but he kept them. Meanwhile that dumb phone is long gone and forgotten, replaced by the new, new thing. Conservatism has a key role to play in the age of future shock, helping to prevent essential institutions from being destroyed in the race toward novelty. Some space should remain for our traditions to survive. With a little care and patience, we can preserve slower, less glamorous values that will enrich us in ways that are difficult to quantify.

A Nation of Millionaires

Why don't we solve all of America's economic problems by simply printing extra money and sending every American a million dollars? It might sound attractive, but it would accomplish nothing. Dump that much money into the economy without creating any additional value, and prices would shift dramatically upward. The next day a cup of coffee would cost $150 and a car might cost $500,000.

What if we did it another way?

What if disruptive new technologies and capital investment radically reduced the man-hours required to complete common tasks? What if the costs of supply-chain management, document storage, energy, business meetings, food production, and hundreds of other necessary human activities plunged over a very short period? What if, instead of giving us all millions of dollars in currency, our political and economic system could make life drastically cheaper on a constantly accelerating time frame? Would the entire revolutionary process escape our attention completely?

Consider this scenario.

In 1985, a top-of-the-line Ford Mustang GT carried a sticker price of $14,000, which, adjusted for inflation, equals roughly $30,000 today. That car featured an AM/FM radio with an optional cassette deck. The finest Mustang you could buy in 1985 had no air bags, no antilock brakes, no remote electronic door locks, no CD player, Bluetooth phone connection, USB ports, or heated seats. It had no cupholders.

Visit a Ford showroom in 2014 and you could drive away with their finest Mustang GT, tricked out with advanced safety features, every gadget imaginable, excellent engineering and reliability, a spectacular warranty, and even cupholders, for roughly $30,000.

Americans have always been relatively prosperous, but just the past generation our collective wealth has grown dramatically. Fueled by the collapse of communism, the global expansion of trade, political liberalization, and mixed-market capitalism, the cost of nearly everything has spiraled downward. Though the impact of this shift has been uneven, this change has at least marginally improved the lives of almost everyone.

The examples could go on and on. In 1985, not even Steve Jobs could afford to store and use all of his music and movies on a device the size of a credit card. Now you can get one on eBay cheaper than the relative cost of a Sony Walkman in the '80s. Overseas travel, electricity, movies, stock trading, even fresh vegetables in the wintertime are cheaper, better, and more broadly available than they were just a generation ago. The only things that are getting more expensive are services that still depend on direct, personalized interaction with a human expert, like health care and education (more on that later).

We often fail to recognize the scope of this new wealth because it falls into a cognitive gap. It hasn't made us rich by our classic definitions. We still have to struggle to have the things we want. We still experience joblessness, foreclosure, and uncertainty. And yet, with each passing year the benefits of financial success become greater and the potential impact of failure are modestly curbed.

Since roughly 1975, the global economy has added more wealth per capita than was created in all of previous human history. The unlocking of the global economy throughout the 20th century produced a staggering explosion of economic growth. Yes, this expansion has been radically unequal, but focusing on that one fact misses an important dynamic that shapes our time.

Understanding this quiet trend toward greater individual wealth would help us understand the global devolution of power away from every traditional center of authority and toward steadily greater individual decision making. Most of all, understanding the impact of the wealth revolution will help us avoid killing this golden goose out of ignorance or fear.

A wealthier, freer world sounds great on paper, but in its wake come new experiences and demands that many find frightening. Freedom sounds great for me, but my neighbor's choices often make me uncomfortable. Some of us unconsciously relish the limitations on our freedoms for the way they limit the burden of decision making, insulate us from cognitive dissonance, and protect us from the outcomes of our choices.

Much worse, our sudden burst of greater individual wealth and freedom is shaking the institutions on which our culture and our political system depend. Recognizing those impacts requires us to peel our attention away from the neighbor who is outearning us and look a little closer at how global capitalism is changing the patterns of risks and rewards in our economy. Not everything is getting cheaper; some surprising things have become radically more expensive.

Haircuts and the Cost of Time

In one generation, radically rising productivity has driven down the cost of almost everything from a long-distance call to a gallon of milk. Less work is necessary to acquire nearly all the things we want, making us effectively richer regardless of income. However, the exceptions to this trend are beginning to expose cultural and political weaknesses.

One outlier is a men's haircut. That's right, a trip to the barber costs nearly 10% more in real terms than it did in 1980. In our magical age, I can watch a movie on my phone, but I still can't download my haircut. And I can't realistically do it myself unless I'm ready to look like a car with the doors left open. In just a few decades we've replaced our stockbrokers and our neighborhood bankers. Many of us have stopped using encyclopedias, stamps, and checks. Fewer and fewer of us hire realtors, carry cash, or listen to the radio.

Nonetheless, in an age of endless technological wonder and personal freedom you still depend on a barber.

Barbers do the same thing they did 30 years ago at pretty much the same pace. No one has invented faster scissors or found a way to trim six heads at once. Your cut can't be outsourced to Mississippi or India. It still demands personal attention from someone with at least a minimal understanding of what they're doing.

The men's haircut sits in the dead zone of our wealth revolution. It illustrates the extent to which our radical economic transformation has made the time and attention of a human being the most valuable commodity on the planet. This cannot be emphasized enough—human beings with some form of skill are more valuable now than they have ever been in history.

Overall, the rising value of human labor is good news. It opens up potential for people to benefit from creativity, hard work, and their efforts to develop themselves. Labor is taking on many of the traditional characteristics of capital. And like capital, human skills that aren't invested or improved upon in some meaningful way yield nearly nothing.

That said, not all labor is increasing in value. Some labor that is tough to automate, like burrito-rolling, hasn't seen any real appreciation. What sets your barber apart from people who work in landscaping or fast food is the expertise required. Granted, the training and knowledge required to wield barber's shears is not as demanding as what it takes to launch satellites, but it still matters just enough for barbers to see the average cost of their work appreciate slightly rather than decline. And for a few, the rewards that flow from achieving mastery of the profession translate into an upper-middle-class income. This is seldom true for your lawn crew.

This has important implications for goods and services we all need. As an example, look at the forces affecting a much higher-value form of labor—medicine.

Your trip to the doctor looks very much like it did 30 years ago, except that your doctor now has very little time for you. The process of delivering medical care could, in principle, benefit from many of the advances in communication, information-sharing, and technology that have slashed costs in other industries, but the densely regulated nature of medicine has made adaptation very slow.

Even with improved efficiency, medical care would still at some level require the direct, personal attention of a skilled professional. Human capital will continue to grow more precious as the wealth revolution advances. What's more, the rising cost of medical care is interlocked with the rising cost of other functions. Our medical infrastructure relies on highly educated doctors who direct care. Education is another product whose costs have been driven up exponentially by the wealth revolution.

Like your barber and your doctor, it is tough to find an automated replacement for the direct, person-to-person attention of a well-trained teacher or professor. Even if costs could somehow be contained, the inherent value of a quality education has risen as our economy has increased the rewards of expert human knowledge. Education at all levels is not only becoming more expensive to produce, it is an increasingly valuable thing to possess, accelerating its rise in price.

You don't have to be a barber, a doctor, or a teacher to find that your time has become more valuable. For those who have successfully converted their labor into capital through education or the development of special skills, time has become tremendously valuable. Not only do we now earn more spending power from a unit of work, the galaxy of options for using our time has increased exponentially.

From our perch in the barber's chair we can catch a distant glimmer of the forces that are changing our politics. Our civic culture is built on a thick bedrock of social capital. Voluntary, personal involvement in myriad institutions has for centuries served to tie us together, temper cultural and political extremes, and strengthen a sense of investment in our common welfare.

We have done almost nothing over the past generation to replace our dependence on social capital, but like education, medical care, and a decent haircut, the personal cost of direct community involvement is rising. Our most crucial institutions are becoming very expensive for us to support. Consequently, they are failing.

The Decline of Social Capital

My suburban Chicago village features a charming old Masonic Lodge in its downtown. More than a century old, the building is a local architectural fixture. It's also a fine commercial office space. The Masons had to sell the place years ago when they could no longer afford to maintain it.

The Masons are not alone. All over the country, you can purchase church buildings at very reasonable prices. Nearly every measure of involvement for community organizations across the country shows steady long-term declines that have accelerated dramatically in the past few decades. The Boy Scouts, PTA, and Rotary Clubs are common examples, but the same dynamic is at work in higher-profile groups.

The rapid expansion of personal freedom and affluence that we have experienced in the past few decades has had a strange economic effect on personal involvement. It has made our involvement in voluntary community organizations radically more expensive.

Thirty years ago, a church-committee meeting might in some sense have been a chore, but it also offered entertainment value. Involvement in local organizations wasn't entirely altruistic. Most households owned one telephone. Opportunities to interact with friends and family were much more localized. There were only three TV stations. If you wanted to watch a movie, you had to schedule a night out or go to the video store. Then, as now, time may have been money, but we had far fewer places to spend or invest it.

Our range of individual choice was also very tightly constrained by social obligations. Tighter communities limited individual decision making. If you didn't pull your share in local organizations, you paid a social toll.

The economic logic of social capital has been turned on its head by our increasing wealth and individual power. Compare the range of choices available on any Tuesday night in 1982 with the options we have now. Compare the range of obligations our neighbors can impose on us now with the ones we faced 30 years ago. We will never go back to those days. Our time is now far more valuable than it has ever been. We are freer to do more things with it that we really enjoy.

A Scout leader summarized the problem nicely in an interview with *The Boston Globe*: "We are in huge competition for kids' time at 7, 8, 9, and 10 years old. It's computers, it's soccer, it's all the activities kids can do." His analysis of children's lives is even more relevant for adults. Compared with people just a generation ago, we have vastly more options for entertainment and involvement.

This is not, on the whole, a negative development. The wealth and freedom that create this conundrum are the realization of a dream once thought impossible, if not absurd.

Some of the personal ties we once fostered through service organizations now develop through other channels. It is easier now to maintain meaningful social connections with friends spread across the country or the world. Our connections are becoming less local, less constrained, and more powerful while our ties with the people who live next door are weakening.

Will we suffer if our communities can no longer support a Woodmen of the World Hall or an Oddfellows Local? What will our culture look like when I choose to spend my evenings posting political rants on Facebook or updating my blog rather than taking my kids to their Scouts meeting or attending a school-board hearing? Perhaps we can live happily in world in which traditional social capital plays a smaller role in our lives. The trouble is, we're in no position to live without a government, and our political system is utterly dependent on social capital.

Our representative government is faltering because it is built on the assumption of broad involvement by people tied together in networks of deep, local, social interaction. As those networks of social capital have eroded, the systems of accountability that served to mitigate extremes and weed out crackpots no longer function as they should. Your local school might be okay with a smaller PTA, but without a rich network of local community organizations, your Congress is coming unglued.

In this atmosphere, a very small number of shockingly irresponsible people can have a disproportionate influence over politics by virtue of their simple willingness to invest their time. We must adapt our bulky, staid, and slow political institutions to the demands of a world in which attention is more precious than money.

The erosion of social capital is going to change the meaning, purpose, and basic capabilities of government in ways that we haven't yet recognized as a culture. The question of how to adapt to this radical social transformation is larger than the mechanics of partisan politics.

Before we can address the ways government must operate differently, we need to recognize the impact of growing wealth and declining social capital on the political process. We have to acknowledge the ways that this decline has empowered vocal, committed minorities who do not always have the best interests of the nation at heart. We need to deal with the growing power of the 1%.

The Power of the Other 1%

"I guess one person can make a difference ... but most of the time they probably shouldn't." — Marge Simpson

Economic and cultural changes have begun to concentrate tremendous power in the hands of a small minority. Our weakening political institutions lack the strength to counter their growing influence. Washington and our state legislatures seem to bow to their every whim, smothering the will of ordinary American voters who feel increasingly alienated from a political process that fails to reflect their values.

Who is really running America? The Koch Brothers? George Soros? The Illuminati? The Lizard People?

Researchers have found the answer: American politics is dominated by "the 1%." The trouble is, this is not the 1% you are expecting. In 2014, the National Journal wrote up polling they conducted with Allstate, and the results are pretty stark. A very tiny minority of people with too much time on their hands compose the overwhelming bulk of political initiative in the U.S.

"Forty-one percent of Americans do not participate very often in any of 10 bedrock activities of American civic and political life, according to the latest Allstate/National Journal Heartland Monitor survey. At the other end of the spectrum, just 1 percent of Americans engage very often in eight or more of the activities—from attending town hall meetings to volunteering in the community to giving money to a cause or political candidate."

It is unfashionable to point this out, but money is vastly overrated as a political force. Some guy who inherited a billion-dollar business certainly has more options to influence political outcomes than the average single mother, but that's nothing new. Money, in the form of political donations, has

30

not been a meaningful factor in the rising wackiness of our politics.

No force in politics is as powerful as the personal investment of time. Direct citizen involvement is the single greatest check on the influence of money in politics. Almost every lever in our political machine is calibrated to favor the opinions of committed individuals who band together to make their voices heard in town halls, caucuses, hearings, conventions, and myriad other formal and informal social networks.

Time, especially the time of capable, skilled individuals, has become the most valuable commodity in our economy, and some people are blessed with more of it than others have. We recognize the growing influence of money because it is easy to understand how money affects politics. We have attempted to construct an entire legal and political infrastructure to document the political activities of the wealthy and keep them in check. We are ignoring the influence of the other elite— those who have precious time to spare and the will to pour it into grassroots politics.

We remain defenseless against the surging power of this other 1 percent. Our politics still leans on institutions too resource-intensive for us to support. And a disturbing proportion of people who are gifted with a wealth of time, and are still willing to invest it in direct political involvement, have too little investment in rational outcomes.

Not so long ago, our politics was deeply influenced by networks of informal mediators. These minor authorities operated at all levels of the process, helping to broker access to the right people. Leadership figures in your local Rotary Club chapter, PTAs, Chamber of Commerce, and churches; local party officials, and others in a vast web of voluntary groups could provide important contacts and help a layman navigate the channels of influence.

Most of these power brokers had no explicit political role. They might be the same people you would ask for a referral to a good lawyer or realtor. Whatever political influence they carried was ancillary to their place in the community. Along the way these intermediaries served as filters. They understood the personal interests of key people in the community. They could sponsor or discourage a proposal or candidate. They could provide advice, support, or warnings. They could tactfully weed out the weird.

These brokers had an inherent moderating influence. They were conservative by nature, declining to challenge established practices or assumptions. But that conservatism was tempered by personal investment. Wherever such networks of social capital flourished (and, by the way, they did not flourish in the South), it was relatively difficult for a few noisy or wealthy interests to exert overweening power.

Wherever a large portion the citizenry was directly involved in supporting local institutions—where networks of social capital were strong—politics was relatively moderate, honest, and pragmatic. Exerting corrupt or lunatic influence there would have been a full-time job requiring enormous investment.

Likewise, it would be difficult in such a scenario to persuade political institutions to back harebrained, self-destructive policies by just ginning up a small mob of weirdoes to pack caucus meetings. There would be too many serious, invested people involved at too many levels of the system for a corps of wingnuts to wield much influence.

The networks of mediators have thinned dramatically as our social-capital infrastructure has withered. Their departure is not necessarily such a bad thing.
There were plenty of reasons not to love this system. It marginalized minority views and, in many cases, minorities themselves. Whereas the South had its very visible Jim Crow laws, discrimination in the North operated mostly through the polite hand of the social-capital infrastructure. As a great

devolution of power erodes the influence of our traditional centers of authority, women, racial and religious minorities, the poor, homosexuals—categories of people who were once limited in public life—have broader economic and political opportunities.

The difficulty is that our political system has been slow to adapt to this transformation. With nothing taking the place of these mediating institutions, politics in many parts of the country is descending into a circus sideshow, conducted less out of duty or commitment than for entertainment or promotion of nonsensical agendas.

We still try to hold caucuses, though in this environment they no longer function in any credible way. Parties still adopt "platforms" even though many of them have become so bizarre that no one considers them meaningful. We haven't found a substitute for the town-hall meeting, so we struggle to make them work.

Nowhere is the growing power of the other 1% more apparent than inside the Republican Party. Why? What is it about Republican politics and history that has left it more vulnerable to cranks? What will happen to the country when the other 1% comes to exert the same kind of influence on the Democratic Party?

Republicans, Democrats, and the Crazy Gap

Both of our main political parties feature some odd characters around the fringes, but it is Republicans, not Democrats, who have been increasingly overwhelmed at the core by goofball politics. The relative vulnerability of the GOP to the forces of crazy may become clearer by examining the fates of the Tea Party and the Occupy Wall Street movement.

The Tea Party movement was a surprise to nearly everyone, especially to the people who set it loose. It began in mundane fashion. For years FreedomWorks, a far-right interest group funded by the Koch brothers, had been training a core of grassroots activists, empowering them with talking points, advice on tactics, and eventually a branding theme: the Tea Party. When a few of the members initiated protests in the wake of President Obama's first inauguration, the organization coordinated coverage of the events with Fox News and its affiliates. A Florida cat lady is generally credited as the first of the FreedomWorks seminar graduates to launch a successful "Tea Party" demonstration, in February 2009, but the protests almost immediately took on a life of their own. Dr. Frankenstein has been struggling to contain the monster ever since.

Occupy Wall Street started out as just another protest. Activists with the Canadian leftist publisher Adbusters planned to stage an "occupation" of Chase Plaza in New York's financial district to express the usual outrage at greed, capitalism, injustice, and ... whatever. Bring your own puppets and guitars. No mimes, please. Adbusters had barely completed their cool poster for the event when they lost control.

Both groups' popularity followed a similar arc, gaining broad initial sympathy that steadily hardened into the usual partisan ruts. Both groups have roots in old extremist traditions. The Tea Party is virtually a carbon copy of the John Birch Society that was aggressively marginalized by establishment conservatives in the early '60s. Occupy Wall Street mirrors the Students for a Democratic Society from the late '60s. Where the two groups differ most starkly is in the impact they've had.

Occupy Wall Street is little more than a footnote, having failed to wield any noticeable influence in Democratic politics. The effort never got past "the opportunity to air societal grievances as carnival," as *The New York Times* described it. The brand was deftly co-opted by the establishment left, which stole its slogan while relegating the Occupy figures themselves to the Island of Misfit Activists, where they sit stewing in their fetid tents.

34

The Tea Party, on the other hand, spread through the Republican biosphere like the zombie virus from *The Walking Dead*. Why would a party dominated by a conservative ideology—an ideology that values tradition, business interests, and slow, organic change be so much more vulnerable to a small corps of dedicated wingnuts than a party packed with leftists, environmentalists, vegetarians, and university professors? What is the origin of the "crazy gap" between the parties and will the gap ever close?

As described in preceding sections, expanding wealth and personal freedom are eroding the social-capital institutions that once served to, among other things, moderate our politics. This is a global phenomenon that affects both of our national political parties. What has set Democratic politics apart from the dynamics of the Republican Party is that "extra-political" groups form the backbone of the Democratic machine. The term refers to organizations with strong political interests, like a state teachers' union, whose main purpose is not inherently political. These groups cannot live on activism alone; they have jobs to do.

Those extra-political groups provide a firewall, at least for a time, against the decline of social capital. There may be fewer people overall participating deeply in political activities, but these institutions still retain enough participation to wield influence. In the Democratic Party, you can push ideology all you want until it bumps up against patronage demands. If the machinery of government stops working, the impact will be felt among the people who control the party's ground operations. Government effectiveness matters to interests at the core of Democratic politics.

In particular, it is the Democrats' lingering domination by two major extra-political institutions—unions and black churches—that forms a bulwark against ideological extremes. Both the unions and the churches are crumbling right along with the other pillars of our social-capital infrastructure, but

35

for a variety of reasons their influence is waning at a slower pace than that of many other institutions.

Take the unions: Unions have a purpose, revenue stream, and membership base independent of (though overlapping with) the Democratic Party's. Though unions' membership is steadily declining, it remains massive in grassroots-political terms, easily the largest organized block in American politics. It has a tight leadership structure capable of disciplining its ranks, and its policy interests are relatively broad compared with groups like the Sierra Club or National Right to Life. Unions played a vital role in hijacking the momentum of the Occupy movement from the anarchists and career protestors that got it started.

Black churches have a similar profile. Though complex, varied and, decentralized, churches have long been the most powerful local political institutions in the African American community. As the repressive conditions of the Jim Crow era recede, a dizzying array of new institutions is emerging to represent the interests of the African-American community, leaving a relatively more modest role for the churches. However, for the time being, black churches remain a crucial vehicle through which local Democratic politics plays out in the precincts.

Their numbers are much smaller than the unions', but their commitment and geographic concentration give the churches a unique capacity to cultivate and steer local power. Their interests are much broader than racial justice; on the whole, they are more driven by community interests than ideological agendas.

Although Democrats draw electoral support from a motley coalition, ranging from affluent progressives to socially conservative blue-collar workers, it is the unions and black churches that make up the core of the party's ground game. A quarter of Democratic convention delegates in 2008 were union members—10% from teachers' unions alone. Another quarter of the delegates were African American (compared with 1.5% at the RNC). That organized, institutionally directed ground force is a trump card in politics. People who walk the precincts, make the phone calls, and drive voters to the polls will have the final say in the policy direction of a political party.

Both the unions and black churches, which control the Democratic ground game, are ultimately much more pragmatic than ideological. The difference this makes can be seen by comparing the styles of two predominantly Democratic organizations, Planned Parenthood and the National Organization for Women.

Planned Parenthood operates women's health clinics all over the country. Those clinics rely heavily on public funding, and therefore public support, and many provide abortion services in areas that are deeply hostile to Democratic politics. The organization has a day-to-day function beyond influencing politics.

NOW, on the other hand, is an issue-advocacy group. Its grassroots activities consist mostly of tracking legislation of concern and mobilizing members to voice support or opposition. It can afford to be as unreasonable as their most generous donors will tolerate. The organization itself is not threatened by any failure to accomplish a practical objective. Advocacy groups feed on controversy. NOW achieving its policy goals would be like a dog catching the car.

For example, NOW took a hard line on the nomination of Supreme Court Justice Samuel Alito, threatening to campaign against otherwise choice-friendly senators from both parties who refused to obstruct his nomination. Planned Parenthood recognized the obnoxious irresponsibility of subverting the democratic process purely to activate a political base. It backed down from a filibuster of Alito's confirmation, angering activists on the extremes but preserving its vital policy influence on Capitol Hill. Planned Parenthood has more to worry about than motivating an extremist base. Planned

Parenthood is no more "moderate" on core issues than NOW, but it is forced to be vastly more pragmatic.

The dominating presence of extra-political organizations like unions, Planned Parenthood, and other groups performing public functions checks the pressure from Democratic activists to pursue irrational extremes. The GOP political universe, by contrast, is made up of dozens of major advocacy groups comparable to NOW, but Republicans have almost nothing like Planned Parenthood, black churches, or unions.

Two forces wield nationwide, multi-interest influence inside the Republican Party. The most important is the loose network of fundamentalist churches and their satellites. They are the only interest groups that can mobilize a national force of grassroots volunteers for conservatives. The modern GOP is dominant where they are numerous and weak where they are thin.

Unlike the unions, the religious right is fragmented, undisciplined, and disorganized. Its disinterest in tangible outcomes and its fascination with the end of the world make dissuading it from pointless and destructive policies tough. Also difficult is mobilizing the group politically through any means other than escalating extremist rhetoric and appeals to fear.

The other institutional force on the right is a narrow cadre of wealthy donors, mostly business and industrial elites. They dominate the donor base, but their influence at the grassroots level is weak and declining. They find themselves in an escalating cycle of spending more to achieve less. With the exception of the Koch brothers and a few other odd characters, they are relatively pragmatic, but they are at the mercy of religious extremists on the ground whom they are increasingly unable to contain.

Neither group is in a position to blunt the extremes. The religious wing doesn't want to, and the business wing can't.

Without some institutional base to provide a moderating influence at the grassroots level and with the local networks of social capital drying up, the Republican Party is becoming a dangerous, though immensely entertaining, catastrophe.

Hardly any traditional Republican interests, apart from perhaps Chambers of Commerce, have a vested material interest in government effectiveness. That leaves no structural force to press back against the entertainers who would motivate turnout in primaries and caucuses with appeals to rabid passions.

There are sensible people involved in Republican politics who sacrifice time they could devote to family, work, or entertainment to participate in politics out of a sense of civic duty. The game is rigged against them. They are outgunned and constantly on the retreat. They have been walking away from day-to-day engagement for decades, when they aren't being actively chased to the margins.

We can talk about solving the problem by encouraging greater grassroots participation by "moderates," but that is a fantasy. The kind of people who care about rational, pragmatic political outcomes are in large part the same people who are busy taking care of their families, their businesses, and the increasingly intense demands of success in America. Even if they, somewhat heroically, chose to carve out time from their jobs and their kids to battle for months for the opportunity to spend all day at Virginia's 2013 GOP nominating convention, would they ever choose to do it again? How many of the sensible people who form the backbone of American life would consistently volunteer to spend weekends in the crowd that nominated Ken Cuccinelli and E. W. Jackson?

This has created a rift between the Republican activist base and the Republican electoral base. If the mechanics of Republican politics continues to favor people with more time than sense, they will nominate fewer and fewer candidates that general election voters will accept. Worse, the traditional core values of the conservative movement will be swamped beneath layers of paranoid muck.

On the other side of the aisle, with both unions and black churches in steady decline, how long can Democrats hold off similar assaults from their irrational left flank? It's impossible to say, but we can be confident that the tipping point is approaching. What will our politics look like when we're forced to choose between a Tea Party candidate in a Ben Franklin costume and a faux-revolutionary Occupier with an iPhone in his raised fist?

As old institutions weaken from the growing shift toward individual independence, wealth, and liberty, the problem of crazy in politics is bigger than either party. We are facing a world in which credible, effective central authority of all kinds is in retreat, with some unanticipated consequences. The growth of personal power is a very good thing, but if it is going to continue, we will have to learn how to contend with its by-products. One core institution being deeply damaged by the collapse of social capital is organized religion.

Disorganized Religion

Anyone who has traveled in Europe may have been surprised at finding only tourists in many beautiful ancient churches. After World War II, religion slipped to the periphery of public life. Europeans are commonly regarded as living in a "post-Christian" age, in contrast to the relative religious enthusiasm of their American cousins. However, the thunder of Bible-thumping from American pulpits may be drowning out the patter of footsteps abandoning the pews. America may be trailing Europe, but it seems to be on the same path.

Travel a few minutes from downtown Houston on the endless lanes of the Southwest Freeway, and you'll find the arena where the Houston Rockets won their NBA championships in 1994 and '95. The last jump ball was thrown there almost two decades ago; the Rockets have moved on to the gleaming

Toyota Center downtown. A new star graces the old arena, bringing in more than 40,000 fans each week. Houston's Summit is now home to Lakewood Church, one of the flagships of the megachurch phenomenon in America.

Churches like Lakewood might seem to represent America's immunity to the religious decline evident in Europe, but look carefully and you'll see a more complex story. As is increasingly typical among American churches, Lakewood is nondenominational. The church operates outside of any larger structure of accountability or organization. It was an entrepreneurial effort by "venture pastor" John Osteen back in the '50s. His heirs own the enterprise. That pattern is repeated over and over again across America's religious landscape.

Attendance figures make clear that churches in America are overall in steady decline, just a few decades behind Europe's. The growth of fundamentalist congregations has not arrested the slide. They seem to act as the exit foyer of organized Christianity, swelling for a time as people leave. Even charismatic denominations like the Southern Baptists, which had benefited from earlier declines in mainline Protestantism, are beginning to see their numbers fall off.

What's emerging in the wake of this decline is a uniquely American brand of post-religious spirituality. The Big Round Church that is replacing America's Little White Churches incorporates Christian themes into an unapologetically consumer-oriented experience. The receding authority of a religious denomination is being replaced by the magnetism of a charismatic pastor, attracting a hardened remnant of fundamentalist believers unconcerned about the moral implications of commercialized faith. Organized religion is giving way to disorganized religion.

Disorganized religion is replacing traditional religious identities with a model in which the customer is always right. It drives an uncompromising line on crowd-pleasing propositions—fiercely condemning broadly unpopular things that "other people" do. Claiming to embrace strictly literal Biblical interpretations, many of these congregations take a literalist approach on homosexual rights, abortion, and the notion that only born-again Christianity can offer a path to salvation and truth. On the other hand, they employ subtle, almost tortured scriptural contortions to avoid being stuck with the less commercially viable by-products of literalism.

Women, who make up half the market after all, aren't required to "remain silent" as the Apostle Paul explicitly demands. Instead, they are popular television preachers and authors. Old Testament admonitions that are perfectly useful to support a hard line on gay rights are toned down where they require the optically unpleasant stoning of disobedient children and blasphemers.

Divorce gets a carefully nuanced treatment, given that a literal line on that subject would be market suicide. The Bible's disappointing failure to make any mention of the vital issue of abortion is overlooked entirely. And Jesus' unreasonable demand that his followers give up their worldly possessions to pursue a life of service is, well, rendered a bit more reasonable. As capitalism slowly converts every cultural institution into a commodity, religious entrepreneurs are turning that doctrinal challenge into a business opportunity.

Thomas Jefferson used a razor to carefully remove all the passages from his copy of the Gospels that mentioned miracles or elements of the fantastic. He discovered in what was left behind a deeply inspiring guide for life, freed from delusions and superstition. Fundamentalists recoil from such a heretical exercise while refusing to put down the knife.

Religion's steady move toward disorganization is a fully global phenomenon. In countries less prepared for the experience, such as Pakistan and Afghanistan, it poses an existential threat while Europe and Canada have walked through it with barely a whisper. The process of religious devolution creates anxiety for many, anxiety that's often displayed in the shape of fanatical extremism and desperate efforts to shore up a disintegrating religious culture by political mandate. We are not immune.

America seems unlikely to suffer as much pain as the Middle Eastern countries have, but it seems unwilling to give up that old-time religion as gracefully as the Europeans. One day the dominant branches of Christianity in America may be as philosophical in outlook as is the bulk of Western Judaism. The mainline Protestant denominations are, for the most part, already on their way. Catholicism may not be far behind. Even the Big Round Church movement, as it begins to grow older, is starting to show some signs of maturity.

Megachurch pastor and author Rob Bell recently drew anger (and lost his job) by embracing a relatively rational interpretation of Hell. Other figures are beginning to think more critically about Biblical approaches to environmental issues and the culture war. These figures remain on the fringes of the evangelical movement, but this is a fringe that did not exist only a few years ago.

Religion isn't going away. It seems to be wired into the fabric of our minds. In the absence of some organized form, we'll construct it out of whatever spare parts we can find. Just spend some time with radical environmentalists to witness a demonstration.

Regardless what else happens to our culture, Christians will likely, for the foreseeable future, continue to gather to discuss the meaning of their faith and build religious communities. They still do this in Europe, though on a much smaller scale than in the past. A mature, disorganized Christianity might grow less enthralled by the fantastic while remaining a significant cultural force. We'll see.

Perhaps one day tourists will quietly marvel at the architectural splendor of our great glass megachurches while token services are carried on in the background. They'll make much better sightseeing stops than the European cathedrals do given that they are already equipped with coffee houses, restaurants, and book stores.

Be sure to stop by the gift shop on the way out.

What is Capitalism?

There is a general agreement that the epic ideological battle between capitalism and communism was won by the capitalists. There is considerably less awareness of what that actually means. We might better manage the tensions we are experiencing in a post–Cold War world if we took a closer look at what capitalism is and what challenges will emerge from its triumph.

Part of the problem is that capitalism, like Christianity, was named by its enemies. None of the great early advocates of capitalist economics—Adam Smith, Alexander Hamilton, John Stuart Mill—would have been familiar with the term. *Capitalism* mostly emerged from late 19th-century Marxists as a pejorative term. Proponents of market economics have never really embraced the term.

Capitalism, however, has a fairly clear logic. The term describes a philosophy about how value is properly and justly assigned. In a capitalist economic and political system, the value of things is determined by the price they can command in an arm's length transaction between a free buyer and seller. From our perspective in the 21st century, this sounds too unremarkable to be adequate as a definition, but this concept was once deeply controversial.

Prior to the emergence of capitalism, value and ownership of assets was determined by tradition, religion, race, and any number of other cultural factors. Ownership of value-producing assets, or capital, was generally assigned based on heredity. The idea of letting an unrestrained market transaction set prices was considered extremely dangerous to society. In fact, it was.

Assigning value based on market transactions opened up unheard-of opportunities for ordinary people to be judged by their productive capacity rather than their class, heritage, religion, or other factors that define one's status in a traditional society. Capitalism is the greatest instrument we have ever devised to generate wealth and alleviate human suffering. Markets and individual liberty tend to accompany each other in the long term, making capitalism extremely dangerous to a system that assigns privileges on the basis of hereditary rights, aristocracy, religion, or some other factor independent of market-defined merit.

Expanding capitalism brought with it an expansion of human dignity, liberty, and prosperity for ordinary people absolutely unparalleled in the history of civilization. Victory means graduating up to better and better sets of problems, but the emergence of unchallenged global capitalism is now presenting problems we did not anticipate.

The power of capitalism hinges on the freedom to eradicate anything that fails to compete in the race toward efficiency. Capitalism is an agent of what economists call "creative destruction."

Creative destruction is not limited to businesses. Markets will tend over time to destroy aristocracies, racial preferences, tradition-based values, religious assumptions, and shared or public resources. It does not matter how valuable something may be in collective or intangible terms. If it cannot hold its own in a commercial transaction between a free, self-interested buyer and seller, it will be devalued, weakened, and eventually swept away.

Market forces that crush racism and aristocracy also eventually threaten institutions we might wish to preserve. Religion, family, tradition, art, and other shared values and institutions that protect our humanity tend to fare poorly in an arms-length market transaction. This is where capitalism faces its own internal inconsistencies. This problem has a name: externalities.

The beauty of capitalism is the remarkable efficiency of markets in setting prices that accurately reflect value. Unfortunately, markets are unable to incorporate values that are "external" to the transaction between an individual buyer and an individual seller.

For example, the market neither knows nor cares whether the goods being traded were obtained by fraud, violence, pollution, or extortion. If a seller is somehow able to produce a cheaper widget by poisoning your well, enslaving homeless children, or simply stealing someone else's widgets, a free market with no government intervention will reward that seller and punish anyone who fails to engage in that commercially optimal but socially despicable behavior.

The problem of externalities also affects the survival of core traditional institutions. What is the value of motherhood? What is the value of religious faith? What is the value of respect for our elders? The deeper capitalism penetrates into a culture, the more its emphasis on commoditization erodes values or institutions that are external to any market transaction, yet essential for the survival of a reasonably humane society.

Markets offer a bright, well-educated mother or father thousands and thousands of dollars to work a full-time job. That same marketplace offers them nothing for raising children other than a series of costly lost opportunities, diminished respect, and serious risks to their future. In an ever broadening competition for time and resources, how can "family values" compete?

The economics of family values is even more brutal for those earning less money. Faced with a choice between helping the kids with their homework in the evening or working a second job that pays just enough to provide everyone with shoes, what decision will a mother or father make? A working mother may want to read to her son at night, but if she has to work the closing shift at Chipotle to retain health insurance, her kids will be on their own. The limited spectrum of decisions that block the working poor from embracing family values serve to the limit the range of decisions open to the next generation.

Capitalism reduces everything to a commodity. If fatherhood, for example, fails to pay enough to compensate for its costs, then it gradually becomes too expensive for anyone to rationally afford. A free market will gradually shift wealth and power to those who abandon the expensive and economically inefficient concept of family values. That's why, until the Cold War, capitalism found itself consistently at war with conservatism. With the fight against communism dead, that old tension is reemerging, though no one seems to recognize it.

The freedom of potential buyers and sellers to reach a price agreement without outside interference is the key to the effectiveness of capitalism. The externalities that such a market fails to account for will eventually destroy the market itself. If I can gain an advantage in a transaction by cheating, theft, or even violence, the market will reward that advantage. Costs created by my behavior remain external to the price of goods on the market unless some powerful force requires an accounting.

Absent government intervention, a free market will keep rewarding violence and theft until those who engage in such practices eventually succeed in shutting down the individual volition that made market conditions possible in the first place. The paradox of capitalism is that its survival is sustained by a partnership between government and markets, a never-ending dance of markets and regulators striving for a balance between "too much" and "not enough" interference.

Markets and governments grow together in constant tension, simultaneously threatening and feeding on each other. That is why government in a market economy is always larger and more sophisticated than the government was in the agrarian society that preceded it (think of the difference between Northern and Southern states in the U.S. prior to the Civil War).

As a market economy grows more complex and dynamic, its demands on collective resources for infrastructure, dispute resolution, and regulation grow with it. Yet markets still need to operate independent of intervention to the greatest extent possible. The relationship between government and a free market is like the relationship between a parent and a teenage child. Capitalism is always chafing at restrictions yet unable to support itself without them.

That brings us back to the old tension between conservatism, in the traditional sense of the term, and capitalism. The beating heart of capitalism is the narrowly self-interested individual in competition with other individuals to wring the maximum commercial value from each interaction. You cannot have unrestrained capitalism and traditional social institutions any more than you can be hot and cold at the same time. The market price of "family values" is very low, and the cost is very high. Without some intervention, noncommercial institutions like churches, community, and family life will die under capitalism.

That is why libertarian author Charles Murray has found traditional values thriving among the affluent and dying among lower earners. The erosion of "family values" that so upsets right-wing religious and political figures like Rick Santorum and James Dobson is a by-product of capitalism. It is not going away. If we love capitalism and we love our traditional institutions, then we must recognize this conflict and build a government capable of balancing the needs of both.

In time, conservatives will likely find themselves moving into partnership with environmentalists and labor in efforts to limit the externalities of capitalism. If you doubt that, take a close look at the politics of one of the world's most conservative institutions, the Catholic Church. At the same time, Hamiltonian Republicans such as Chris Christie and David Brooks will probably shift into alignment with traditional liberals in defense of markets and personal freedom.

Many political earthquakes stand between today's political parties and a durable post–Cold War realignment. Until that rocky transition is complete, our politics will remain a muddled mess and Washington may be dogged by gridlock. The sooner we all come to remember the meaning of terms like *conservative* and *capitalist*, the faster we can complete this uncomfortable transition.

The American Devolution

We have entered an era of relentless creation and destruction that is shifting power in every form away from established elites, devolving it into smaller and smaller cores. This force has been in motion in the West at least since the time of the printing press. Our republic was an early product of this great devolution of power.

But with the radical advances in technology over the past two generations, this shift has accelerated exponentially, leading to a sort of atomization of power. On the whole this is a good thing. It means that human labor has become the most valuable commodity on Earth, and as a result, the old elites who hoarded power and the benefits it brought are seeing their influence weaken. Like any good thing, this massive devolution is pulling some dangers in its wake. As the pressure builds globally on the staid old institutions of politics, this wave of transformation is beginning to threaten the very existence of government as we know it.

Our economy has already been transformed by the new normal of constant, radical change. Look at what's happened over just the past few years to the music industry, video stores, even Internet Age businesses like dial-up Internet service providers. Entire industries, not just companies, have been born and obsolesced over the course of my own professional career.

Government by its very nature is slower than business to adapt, and the pressure is mounting. Individuals have more power than they have ever possessed before. Our culture and economy have become far too dynamic for anyone to hope to control. Government hasn't become obsolete, but in its current design it lacks the flexibility to do its job effectively. In many places, the failure of government institutions to keep pace with new challenges is creating a spiral of failure and collapse.

In places like Somalia and Haiti, these forces have led to the complete breakdown of civil authority. Other weak governments—such as those in Afghanistan, Iraq, Libya, Syria, and Congo—have practically ceased to function outside a few key cities. Strategically crucial nations like Pakistan and Egypt are teetering on the brink of chaos. Even in stable, established Old Europe, the Belgians recently lived for nearly two years with no elected government. The long trend toward devolution is beginning to topple some dominoes.

At home in the U.S., it is possible to find areas of government that have effectively collapsed. Here's a test: Call emergency services in Detroit to report a property crime, then monitor the time it takes for an officer to respond. You might want to have a sandwich ready. And a place to sleep.

Sections of downtown Birmingham, Alabama, look like postwar Germany. The bankrupt local government is struggling to cope with the scourge of abandoned buildings and decaying infrastructure, including a beautiful old downtown bank in ruins. Once-vibrant cities like Buffalo, New York; Dayton and Cleveland, Ohio; and Jackson, Mississippi, are shrinking rapidly, creating an expensive spiral of serious budget and infrastructure problems. A new landscape of American ghost towns is emerging as economic dynamism accelerates.

Power is shifting rapidly away from the collective institutions that once formed the basis of our world. We are seeing individuals take on far greater individual wealth, power, and decision-making authority. This is good. In fact, it is the realization of a long human dream and the result of much bloodshed and struggle. However, progress means graduating up to better and better problems, and they will need to be addressed if we are to place the next generation in a position to enjoy the same benefits we have.

Old, organized centers of authority, whether religious, political, or economic, have grown brittle as individuals acquire greater power. This devolution of power could be dangerous if we do not adapt. The collapsing influence of old authorities like organized religion, business leaders, and political institutions has a general destabilizing effect, undermining our ability to manage our collective affairs.

Some on the far right might stand up and cheer at the trend toward weaker centralized institutions, but a sudden, disorderly transition away from the past will be good for no one. Seeing Lycos, for example, rise from nothing to become a $5.4 billion company and then disappear, all in less than a decade, may be interesting. But government is a bit more important to civilization than a search engine. If it faces the same fate, we will all pay dearly.

Government, in its present form, is what keeps our civilization functioning with a relatively low level of violence. It gives us the freedom to engage in economic activity without the constant threat of theft or coercion. It prevents us from having our capital investments destroyed by more-powerful forces that would pollute, monopolize, or defraud their way to an unstoppable advantage. Without it, we get to live like Somalis.

Or, perhaps more importantly to some, without it you will not get your Netflix on time, not even on your iPad.

In an atmosphere this dynamic, the big, bureaucratic central governments of the 20th century cannot function effectively. We need a bridge to a smaller, more flexible, less intrusive government, and we need to cross that bridge without Washington erupting in flames. And we need to do it quickly—within a generation.

Getting Over the "Middle Class"

If it seems like America's middle class isn't what it used to be, perhaps that's because it doesn't exist anymore. The shift toward a vastly more dynamic economy has had serious consequences for the great American middle. There is no longer a coherent block of Americans in the middle income range that shares a culture, goals, and an identity. In other words, the middle class as our central economic driver and cultural lodestone is gone.

Whether that's a good thing or a bad thing will depend on whether we are willing to adapt to the demands of this new reality. With time and reflection, we may find that the middle class, like the family farm, is something fondly remembered only because we selectively forgot the gory details. Good or bad, it's likely to take us a long time to come to terms with this unsettling development.

Adapting to the decline of the middle class will not be easy, in part because the middle class is such an utterly sacred American myth. Speaking honestly about the end of the middle class will be like calling someone's baby ugly.

So, about that baby ...

Let's start by trying to identify the middle class, not just as an economic reality but also in terms of its cultural meaning. Then let's look closely at the long decline in the share of national income going to middle earners. Finally, let's revisit our assumption that the middle class as a concept is too gosh-darned swell for us to live without. Maybe, just maybe, the baby really is ugly. Maybe, for all its daunting challenges, the post-middle-class era offers a chance to build a better way of life than we experienced before.

Economists might define the middle class by measuring relative incomes, but "middle income" as represented in spreadsheets has never quite lined up cleanly with the "middle class" archetype lodged so stubbornly in American heads. In strictly economic terms, the middle class could be defined as the households whose earnings place them in the middle three quintiles of annual earnings—the middle 60%. When we look at their earnings over time, it becomes clear that the myth of America as a country driven by middle-earning households with a common cultural identity may have been true once, but only very briefly during the postwar doldrums of the 1950s.

In that period, incomes for most people who worked for a living were bunched in a relatively narrow range. Middle-income earnings as a percentage of overall GDP peaked in 1957, at nearly 55%. The percentage of the nation's income earned by middle-earning households has been declining ever since in an almost uninterrupted straight line.

Since the '50s, the share of national income earned by the households in the middle has declined by more than one-fifth overall, dropping 5% just since 2000. The middle is no longer king in economic terms, but the cultural erosion has been even stronger.

For Americans, the middle class is not so much an economic marker as a symbol of our civic religion. Only about 12% of Americans define themselves as something other than "middle" or "working" class. *Middle class* for Americans is shorthand for *ordinary folk* or just *us*. Economists can define the term in way that seems to make some loose empirical sense, but the middle class in America less a measured reality than an ideal.

Our vision of a middle-class existence is an expression of our ideas about fairness and our unique relationship to the notion of equality. Under the middle-class ideal, no one need experience poverty or rely on welfare so long as they are willing to work. Americans do not believe in equality as a natural state so much as an achievement. It is considered an axiom of American life that a willingness to work for money is the gateway to this rarefied realm of equality and civic righteousness—the middle class.

The common interests that once made middle earners a "class" were cultural, not just economic. Many bankers, lawyers, plumbers, and factory workers lived in cookie-cutter houses in the same neighborhoods as one another. Almost all of them had done mandatory service in the military, forging a bond of common experience and exposure to a national identity. The lawyer might be marginally more likely to drive a new car, but the features of his vehicle wouldn't have varied much from those of the plumber's. Differences in lifestyle were subtle.

That commonality is gone. We can still identify a middle class of sorts by bracketing households that earn roughly the median income. Someone will always sit in the middle. However, apart from income, that cohort of people will share few of the overlapping interests that define a class. Our civilization has diverged into dozens of identifiable cohorts that cross and re-cross each other on certain criteria or at certain stages of life, but mostly they just seem to be heading in a thousand different cultural directions.

Two things killed the American middle class: global capitalism and the civil-rights movement. In some sense, the middle-class era perished from its own success. It is being replaced by something freer, more dynamic, and more authentically based in our founding notions of equality and liberty.

The decline of the middle class, as measured by income statistics, is often blamed on increasing wealth concentration among the highest earners. But a focus on the 1%, and the rest of the upper class, obscures a potentially more important trend. The changes in America's income structure and class alignment may have less to do with *concentration* than with *shearing.*

Income statistics show that over time middle earners' fortunes have diverged. Professionals and information workers have seen their share of the national income increase while the economic value of manual labor has sagged. It is true that the top 5% of households have seen the greatest increase in their income share since the late '50s. However, the same phenomenon has led to a rising share of national incomes for roughly the top third. Possibly the largest beneficiaries of America's shift toward global capitalism are white-collar professionals. Fifty years ago they earned barely more than their neighbors who worked at the factory. Now they more closely aligned with wealthier households.

Perhaps America has no middle class because, for a very large portion of the population, the values and goals of the middle class worked. The sacrifices and achievements of a prior generation launched millions of Americans from what had been the middle class into this new reality of higher incomes, more-dynamic careers, and vastly greater options. More people than ever before are experiencing real affluence.

There is more happening here than just a shift in earnings. Professional workers experience career patterns and relative job security more in line with high-income households. In 2012, with the economy still struggling, the unemployment rate for IT workers was about 3%—well beyond the technical bound of full employment. In fact, unemployment for knowledge workers and other professionals hovered at about half the broader unemployment rate for most of the downturn. Not only are knowledge workers earning more than their blue-collar peers, their career arc, retirement expectations, and relative security are a world apart from those of traditional labor.

But as these workers have graduated into a new, more affluent way of life, they have left behind a large number of formerly middle-class Americans who are seeing their lifestyles deteriorate. And although knowledge workers in the top 10th to 33rd percentiles of households have become closely aligned culturally with higher earners, they share little economically with the wealthy. Affluent workers in that income set are far more sensitive to tax increases than are the truly wealthy in the highest income tiers. We often imagine that the super-wealthy are blocking efforts to raise taxes, but much of the meaningful political resistance is coming from the higher end of the middle incomes.

This economic realignment can't be blamed on Reagan or Bush. Every president since Eisenhower has presided over a creeping erosion in the share of national income earned by the middle quintile. This phenomenon is far bigger than tax policy. In fact, it is bigger than America.

All across the developed world, income inequality is rising. Western Europe has been experiencing rising inequality since the '80s despite a dense social-welfare network. Sweden, of all places, is experiencing one of the steepest expansions in the percent of national wealth consumed by the richest few.

Policy is a component of rising inequality, but it is not the *trigger*. Inequality is driven by the same structural factors that are fueling economic dynamism. A free, globalized economy rewards those who can accumulate either capital or knowledge, or both. Progressive taxation may blunt inequality around the edges and help fund programs that expand opportunity. However, if conceived purely as a means to halt income concentration, higher marginal rates are just boulders in the stream. The radical expansion of freedom and economic opportunity that has swept the whole planet during the past half century has disproportionately rewarded those who can accumulate knowledge and capital, and will continue to do so no matter how (within reason) we change tax rates.

A knowledge economy is bent toward extreme outcomes. Nassim Nicholas Taleb has described this as the central characteristic of life under conditions he labels "Extremistan." In short, a globalized knowledge economy magnifies the rewards that accrue to outliers in certain kinds of enterprises.

Your accountant or your yoga instructor may experience an economy not much different than in the past. An accountant can process only so many tax returns in a given season. Likewise, a yoga instructor can personally tutor only so many people at a time. Advances in communications technology may provide some help at the margins, but for the most part they don't affect these workers.

On the other hand, your town's favorite band is experiencing the dynamics of Extremistan. Recorded music faces no limitations of geography or scale. In the Information Age it no longer even requires a physical medium for delivery. A few very successful artists can capture a massive share of the overall market, leaving little room for the best band in your town to compete against the best band in the world. As the knowledge economy accelerates, all kinds of professions that we never imagined might be subject to automation or globalization are experiencing the dynamics of Extremistan.

Can we preserve the ideals of middle-class America in an age of rising economic inequality? Probably not, but before we try, we should consider whether that's even a good idea. We've seen how capitalism has undermined the middle class. What about the effect of the civil-rights movement?

Think for a moment about depictions of middle-class life in culture. The mind perhaps conjures images from *Leave It to Beaver* or The *Andy Griffith Show*. We think of harmonious two-parent families settled in lovely quiet homes with manicured lawns. But more-realistic depictions can be found in the AMC series *Mad Men,* or the book and subsequent film *The Man in the Gray Flannel Suit.* Better yet, temper that memory of middle-class America by reading *To Kill a Mockingbird* or *Silent Spring.*

Life at the height of the middle class was racially segregated, sexist, and cruelly obsessed with conformity. Our environment was more polluted than it has ever been. Personal choices were relentless constrained, partly by law but even more stringently by cultural pressures. At the peak of middle-class wealth and influence, our culture was insular, paranoid, and repressive.

Blacks, Hispanics, and women had no space to participate independently in the economy, politics, or culture. Jews and even Catholics also faced barriers to participation and influence. Any potentially disruptive cultural or economic force was stubbornly repressed. No one should be surprised at the rebellion that ensued or the decline in middle-class power that followed.

We generally recognize the impact of the civil-rights movement on racial minorities while often neglecting its impact on others who were marginalized. The civil-rights movement began as an effort to gain political equality for African-Americans, but it blasted open our culture, making it possible for the first time for non-white, non-male Americans to be evaluated in public life on the basis of their relative merits rather than their inherited status. Once that barrier was broken, the stultifying cultural uniformity of middle-class America was doomed.

We have little to gain from battling this dynamic and cramming people back into some ersatz vision of middle-classness. Extremistan may be uneven in its outcomes, but it is delivering lifestyle options that we'd never imagined for nearly everyone.

We may decide to wave goodbye to the cultural myth of the middle class, but we must act to mitigate—not to stop—the inequality that is emerging in the wake of its demise. Our goal in coping with the end of middle-class America should be to preserve meaningful equality of opportunity in an era of vast economic and cultural dynamism. In particular, we need to find ways for those in lower-income households to get a solid shot at participating in the knowledge economy. The challenge of a post-middle-class America is preserving opportunity, not re-imposing conformity or manufacturing some phony equality.

Preparing for that challenge starts with ditching the old way of characterizing economic strata. There is no middle class to which political figures can appeal. Shearing and cultural liberalization have destroyed it. Pretending that a middle class still exists can wreak political havoc. Perhaps the best example of this came in early 2015.

When President Obama announced plans to grant tuition-free access to community colleges, his idea immediately ran into a massive and unanticipated obstacle. The administration had proposed to pay for subsidized community-college tuition by removing the tax-exempt status of college-savings plans (known as 529 plans).

What administration officials seemed to think they were doing was building a bold proposal to help the middle class. What they tripped over was the new fault line in our culture between those who have benefited from global capitalism and their poorer cousins in the lower-middle-income tiers. The funding plan was dead within a couple of weeks.

That unappreciated divide stands in the way of nearly every sensible effort to expand opportunity to lower-income families. Making public-school funding more equitable, expanding subsidies for child care, making higher education more accessible to low-income or minority students—the political power that's blocked these measures has not come from the very wealthy, but from the beneficiaries of the death of middle America. Dual-income families pulling in $200,000 to $400,000 a year are the most threatened by these reforms and have worked hard to thwart them.

They are relatively wealthy, but they still work for a living, they often live paycheck to paycheck, and their lives and hopes are very sensitive to changes in tax policy. Many still think of themselves as "middle class," and most of their parents genuinely were. Their political heft has grown along with their incomes, but they are almost universally blind to the impact of their choices on their cousins who didn't get into State U.

Most dangerously, they seem to view themselves as the beneficiaries of a new meritocracy rather than the survivors of a shipwreck. Blissfully unaware of the ways that a previous era of white domination put them at the front of the line for all of our society's most valuable resources, many regard themselves as "self-made." Armed with superior resources and influence, they are blocking off routes to competition in education and other areas.

A knowledge economy promises massive returns for those who can obtain the training and education to participate. Education has become a threshold for access to that economy.

No one shows up one day to take a test and then gets admitted to Georgetown. Talent helps, but for a talented young person to even get in line to compete for a higher education now requires years of conditioning. Ten-year-olds do not innately know and select the public schools, clubs, tests, and classes that would put them in that line. Their place is fixed early, often at birth. America cannot continue to compete in an increasingly flat world if the only talents we are willing to develop are those of people born into the shearing class.

Acknowledging the death of the middle class is not a surrender, but a crucial step toward building something better. Middle earners are not a class. Their interests are not aligned. If we continue to pretend that a middle class exists, or should exist, we will continue tripping blindly over unseen obstacles in our effort to build better policy.

Liberated from our assumption that most people should be bunched together in the economic and cultural middle, we might have a chance to create a far freer world, one that is more open to individual choices and less vulnerable to economic disasters. By making some intelligent choices, we may one day look back on the end of the middle-class era not as a failure, but as the stepping stone to something far greater than we can imagine.

Getting to that point will not be easy. Before we can we evaluate potential paths, we have to a look a little closer at the ways that the powerful dynamism of a capitalist economy is changing the shape of our future. Leaving behind the outdated myths of the middle class requires us to begin to envision something better.

Grappling with Exponential Growth

Since the '60s, analysts have been using Moore's Law to summarize the expansion of computing power and, by extension, the growth of information technology as an industry. Named for Intel co-founder Gordon Moore, this "law" can be summarized to state that computing power per dollar spent can be expected to double every one to two years.

Moore himself expected the phenomenon to hold for a decade or so in the early life of the computer industry, but it remains fairly consistent 40 years later. If anything, there are signs that this phenomenon may actually be accelerating. Though computing based on silicon chips may struggle to keep up with Moore's Law, the introduction of quantum computing and even biocomputing may soon make Moore's Law seem quaint.

The authors of the recent book *The Second Machine Age* argue that one of the challenges of adapting to this new economic reality is our mental struggle to comprehend the power of exponents. They illustrate the point with a reference to an Indian folktale:

"As the story goes chess was invented by a very clever man who traveled to Patliputra, the capital city, and presented his brainchild to the emperor. The ruler was so impressed by the difficult, beautiful game that he invited the inventor to name his reward.

"The inventor praised the emperor's generosity and said, "All I desire is some rice to feed my family." Since the emperor's largess was spurred by the invention of chess, the inventor suggested they use the chessboard to determine the amount of rice he would be given. "Place one single grain of rice on the first square of the board, two on the second, four on the third, and so on," the inventor proposed, "so that each square receives twice as many grains as the previous ...

"If his request were fully honored, the inventor would wind up with 2 to the 64th power, or more than 18 quintillion grains of rice. A pile this big would dwarf Mount Everest; it's more rice than has been produced in the history of the world."

What's truly fascinating about this process is the way the growth curve bends upward on the *second half of the chessboard*. This is not a bell-curve phenomenon, but a launch.

Why does computing follow a steeper growth curve than earlier technologies did? The chessboard analogy helps us recognize that this is a misunderstanding of the situation. Computing isn't such a unique technology as compared with, say, the steam engine. The difference is that computing is arriving on the second half of the chessboard.

Looking at the growth of technology across all of human history, almost nothing happened until about 1750. The development of fire, agriculture, and the wheel were thousands of years apart. Gunpowder came along another few thousand years later. Steam and mechanical technology were farther along this curve, but they still emerged relatively early.

It's not that computers are so special. It's where they fall on this general expansion of knowledge that makes them more dynamic than previous technologies. And seeing the growth of technology along this long time frame, we begin to recognize that this phenomenon is not about computing at all, and that it is likely to accelerate from here in ways that our brains can barely process.

What this means beyond computing can perhaps be illustrated with a look at the industries spawned by this expansion in computing power. Again, from *The Second Machine Age*:

"The ASCI Red, the first product of the U.S. government's Accelerated Strategic Computing Initiative, was the world's fastest supercomputer when it was introduced in 1996. It cost $55 million to develop and its one hundred cabinets occupied nearly 1600 square feet of floor space at Sandia National Laboratories in New Mexico. Designed for calculation-intensive tasks like simulating nuclear tests, ASCI Red was the first computer to score above one teraflop—one million floating operations per second—on the standard benchmark test for computer speed. By 1997 it had reached 1.8 teraflops ...

"Nine years later another computer hit 1.8 teraflops, but instead of simulating nuclear explosions it was devoted to drawing them and other complex graphics in all their realistic, real-time, three-dimensional glory. It did this not for physicists, but for video game players. This computer was the Sony Playstation 3 ... The ASCI Red was taken out of service in 2006."

It took humans about 3,000 years to move from ox-driven plows to mechanical plows. In fact, agricultural technology at the time of the American Revolution was no better, and in some regards perhaps less advanced, than that used by the Romans. By contrast, we went from Pong to Halo in 25 years.

Why does this matter politically? This kind of growth is a major adaptive challenge for traditional institutions. We need them more than ever, but they groan and occasionally fail under the strain. Government built to meet the bureaucratic demands of 20th-century industrial capitalism is struggling to remain not just relevant, but intact.

Industrialization destroyed an old political order based on aristocracy and land ownership. How will automation transform our current order? And why doesn't this growth show up in our economic metrics?

The rate of economic growth, as measured in terms of GDP, has been on a long, slow decline in the West since the 1960s. Meanwhile, technology is advancing at a pace so fast, it seems that only children have the time to stay current. The authors of *The Second Machine Age* point out that digital-age economic progress looks like stagnation when measured by traditional means.

"We measure economic growth in terms of production and consumption. There is nothing in our economic calculus that measures improvements in well-being, happiness, health or satisfaction. Whatever increases productivity or units of consumption is good. Anything that decreases consumption or production is bad."

While economic "growth" in the Western world has looked relatively flat, our quality of life has improved by nearly every measure. Most of the benefit of the computer age escapes our traditional economic measures entirely. In fact, on paper much of it looks like economic contraction. Take the music industry as an example. Once again, from *The Second Machine Age*:

"Music is hiding itself from our traditional economic statistics. Sales of music on physical media declined from 800 million units in 2004 to less than 400 million units in 2008 ... Before the rise of the MP3, even the most fanatical music fan, with a basement stacked high was LP's, tapes, and CD's, wouldn't have had a fraction of the twenty millions songs available on a child's smartphone via services like Spotify or Rhapsody ... If you're like most people, you are listening to more and better music than ever before.

What has been the impact of this spectacular improvement in lifestyle? By traditional metrics, the introduction of digital music has been economic catastrophe. The value of music has not changed, only the price. From 2004 to 2008, the combined revenue from sale of music dropped from $12.3 billion to $7.4 billion—that's a decline of 40%. Even when we include all digital sales, throwing in ringtones on mobile phones for good measure, the total revenues to record companies are still down 30%. Similar economics apply when you read the New York Times, Bloomberg Businessweek, or MIT Sloan Management Review online at a reduced price or for free instead of buying a physical copy at the newsstand ... Analog dollars are becoming digital pennies."

Overall, what has been the value of making dictionaries, news, music, encyclopedias, health information, and other formerly expensive products free or virtually free? Our lives have been meaningfully enriched and our productivity improved. Yet the impact to economic growth in traditional consumption-oriented terms has been almost entirely negative. Again from the book:

"A simple switch to using a free texting service like Apple's iChat instead of SMS, free classifieds like Craigslist instead of newspaper ads, or free calls like Skype instead of a traditional telephone service can make billions of dollars disappear from companies' revenues and the GDP statistics."

It is extremely difficult to reduce the lifestyle improvement delivered by the iPhone or improved medical-imaging technology or the self-driving car to a metric. What this means is that the most radically concentrated improvement in human life and happiness that has ever occurred in our history is happening with remarkably little notice. By failing to note this transformation, we are missing many of the opportunities presented by this era to improve our lives even further.

Think back to the 1985 Ford Mustang described in an earlier section. A brand-new Mustang sells for slightly less in inflation-adjusted terms than the best Mustang available in 1985. The new one includes such a galaxy of advanced features that the two vehicles can hardly be compared to one another. In GDP terms, the new Mustang represents a decline in economic output. The advent of disruptive new technologies that radically improve our lives have a depressive effect on economic growth as we traditionally measure it.

We are living longer, healthier lives with better access to quality food, information, transportation, art, literature, entertainment, and almost anything else we desire. Those advantages are compounding at a fantastic rate, changing what it means to be rich, poor, and everything in between. Almost none of this shows up in our traditional calculations of economic growth or progress, and much of it is actually depressing our growth metrics.

We would be wise to revisit our assumptions about what computers can and cannot do. Many of us were surprised at the development of computers that could defeat a human at chess or on the game show *Jeopardy!* Although those achievements were novel, we still understood that certain tasks remained essentially human. Computers follow an algorithm, but they do not learn, or adapt to scenarios they were not programmed to see.

In *The Second Machine Age*, the authors illustrate the remarkably rapid crumbling of barriers to automation with a ride in a Google car. Only a few years ago, the pursuit of self-driving automobiles was practically abandoned following a series of humiliating failures. Driving is a task that is not only computationally challenging, it is filled with surprises that cannot be programmed. Driving is the kind of pattern-recognition task that was generally assumed to lay beyond the reach of automation.

Now Google regularly has visitors picked up from the airport in fully automated vehicles. The company's progress in this area is sufficiently advanced that it has moved its efforts into the regulatory sphere, working to pass state laws ensuring that its technology can be deployed on the road.

And that's not all. The folks at Narrative Science are automating journalism. This is not some distant goal of experiments in a lab. A significant portion of what you read today, especially in sports and financial reporting, is generated by the computers at Narrative Science. Their software combs through a data feed searching for relevant elements, then assembles them into a fully developed, publishable story. This gives a news organization, or a data analyst, access to more content than ever.

Narrative Science's software and other, similar big-data tools do not eliminate journalists, but they change what a journalist does. That process stands to radically reduce the number of jobs in the field while making the jobs that remain vastly more lucrative and interesting.

Gone are the days of typing up box scores or summarizing last night's arrests. A journalist using a big-data feed is looking for meaning, not content—that's a good summary of what high-value employment looks like in the second machine age. A journalist, in this context, is leveraging a machine to reduce drudgery, easing the challenge of finding value amid a stream of data.

Similar roles in other fields will provide rewarding work training machines to perform new tasks, leveraging machines to solve new problems, and interpreting new machine output. Those who work with machines are increasingly artists, whether in the literal sense or merely in the shape of their work. Software developers and Daft Punk alike have found success in the second machine age by marrying creativity to automation.

Artists and entertainers were once poor almost by definition. The transition we've seen over the past half century has been so dramatic, we've largely forgotten that for all of human history, performers were social outcasts, the lowest of the low. Celebrity culture is in many ways a by-product of the second machine age, not just because the bounty of this phenomenon creates more disposal income to be used for entertainment. Almost everything humans do successfully in this environment is at its core a creative or artistic pursuit.

The winners in the second machine age are all in some sense artists, whether they post their work on YouTube, GitHub, or *The New York Times*. Liberal-arts degrees may deserve more respect than we've been giving them. The only job category that is reasonably secure from automation, at least for the near term, may be poetry.

Automation is likely to eliminate the job I did yesterday. In doing so, however, it could open up work that I never imagined might exist. That work will likely be more independent, with a less certain future but more-spectacular earnings than we have come to expect. It will also likely lead to shorter careers that start later, often preceded, interrupted, and followed by exploratory ventures that may or may not pan out.

This transition from the boring reliability of Industrial Age employment toward the terrifying excitement and reward of the digital age is completely transforming our understanding of what government can and should do in the economy. We need to think a little harder about how to adapt our institutions to support our values in a rapidly transforming world.

An Economy of Extremes Is Changing the Meaning of a "Job"

The software company VMware, which was founded in 1998, had in 2014 roughly the same market value as General Motors. As of early 2014, VMware had 13,000 employees. GM employed almost a quarter of a million people. In addition to its current workforce, GM supports roughly half a million retired workers through its pension and health-insurance programs. VMware supports zero retired employees.

Tight, accelerating cycles of deeply disruptive innovation are the defining characteristic of economics in our age. Global capitalism has brought us many wonderful things, including vast new freedom, wealth, and security. These benefits have been accompanied, however, by extremes.

Each member of VMware's much smaller workforce earns much more on average than employees at GM ever did, but that isn't the story. Looking closely, you find that a relatively large percentage of the software company's employees pull down annual earnings that would have made a GM executive in the '60s or '70s blush with embarrassment. Knowledge-economy jobs provide highly variable, often very lucrative opportunities to earn far more than workers with similar levels of education and background would have in the past.

The result is a strange dual economy. On one side of the divide is the large minority of the workforce, perhaps 20%–25% (so far), who make their way into information professions. They tend to start their "serious" careers much later and end them much earlier than has previously been common. They may not earn enormous amounts of money every year, but they have an unusual opportunity for the big hit—a stretch of a few years in which they earn a very large income, or the right job with a start-up company that yields millions.

Even those who do not experience a massive windfall generally manage to accumulate enough money across a 20-year career that they can make the transition from working for labor to earning money from capital. In essence, for the first time ever we have a significant mass of the workforce whose labor functions like capital.

On the other side of the divide are workers who remain in conventional careers, still a majority of the workforce. The lucky ones, perhaps in government jobs or protected industries, will see steady though lackluster earnings, enough to maintain a middle-income lifestyle and accumulate enough money for a form of retirement. They will constantly dodge layoffs, downsizing, and privatization. Success will mean a lifetime of well-played career defense.

All around them will be peers, family members and former colleagues, who either made the shift into knowledge careers or fell off the ladder because of layoffs or the toll of strain. For those who lose traditional jobs, career options are dim. The economy offers little in the way of steady employment without a strong education.

Service-sector jobs are generally available, but few of them provide the earnings required to support a family. Almost none of them provide the access to health insurance necessary to support a family over time. Many families in these situations manage to hold themselves together until someone's illness delivers the breaking blow. Absent any meaningful safety net or access to insurance, all too many fall into poverty with its attendant problems.

Whether we mean to or not, we are deciding now on the shape of a post-jobs economy. What will American culture, politics, health care, and economics look like in an era when the "steady job" has ceased to be the most common way that Americans earn a living?

This is not just a question of how we treat the less fortunate, those who do not find jobs in shiny new tech start-ups. The post-jobs economy is not necessarily an unemployment economy. The shift away from formal employment does not mean stagnation or idleness.

One of the surprising options for workers in traditional employment who see their jobs disappear is to become their own boss. Sometimes this takes the form of contract employment, perhaps even more grueling than their previous work. But the dynamics of this economy make entrepreneurship very attractive for those few who have the support system to allow it.

More and more Americans are shedding formal employment in favor of more-flexible work arrangements or starting their own businesses. Since 1990, small businesses and solo ventures have accounted for <u>twice as many new jobs</u> as large enterprises. Yes, many people are falling behind in the competition for knowledge-based jobs, but that is neither the only, nor necessarily the dominant theme of the knowledge economy.

The Affordable Care Act was billed by opponents as a "job killer," but even in the early stages of its implementation it is having a surprising impact on entrepreneurship. With greater access to health insurance outside formal employment, people are beginning to take risks on small ventures that were too dangerous before because of the risks of going uninsured.

The dynamics of the knowledge economy, much higher wages for professionals combined with the deflationary force of innovation, are creating shorter, more flexible careers and more opportunity for entrepreneurship. For those who avoid falling into the dangerous chasms opened up by this economic realignment, the knowledge economy promises a freer, more prosperous world. The key to this future will be adapting our political arrangements to narrow those chasms and to update the safety net beneath them.

Decisions we make now about health care, education, and the shape of the social safety net will not only affect the poor, they will determine how many Americans can afford the kind of risk-taking that accompanies entrepreneurship and innovation. There is an opportunity hiding in this transition. If we can shed the notion that government equals slavery, we could use a modified social safety net to unlock a massive economic expansion and a radical shift toward greater real personal independence than we have ever before experienced.

It is important to remember that this economic transformation is a global phenomenon. The nation that experiences the greatest success in harnessing economic dynamism without creating a desperate underclass will dominate the next century. We have every reason to be the winners in this race. A bright future awaits if we have the courage and intelligence to seize it.

The Food-Truck Future

A food fight emerged in Houston in 2013, between the local restaurant lobby and mobile operators. Food-truck vendors were looking for relief from a set of city operating rules crafted to protect the interests of downtown restaurant owners.

Houston is a surprising venue for a failed effort to limit protective government regulation. Neither the city, with more than 2 million residents, nor the county, with more than 4 million, has any zoning laws. Houston is perhaps America's singular experiment with urban libertarianism, yet protective regulation remains popular even among the region's powerful political right. The challenges facing small-scale, disruptive entrepreneurs in Houston are a benchmark for the wider economy.

Beneath the greasy smokescreen of arguments about safety hid a very simple question that the Houston City Council had to answer: Is it right for the city to explicitly promote one safe, responsible business model over another? By leaving its regulations in place, America's capital of urban libertarianism chose to protect existing businesses from competition. More broadly, this preference for incumbents is dampening the ability of small-scale entrepreneurs to benefit from a more dynamic economy.

The food trucks in this fight are not the ones I used to welcome while working at the junkyard or on a construction site. In recent years, innovative chefs have developed a new business model transforming the traditional restaurant concept, radically lowering the capital requirements to enter the business. This means that chefs can make a living on a far lower turnover, freeing them to experiment with ingredients, products, and quality in ways that the relatively high-capital standard restaurant model made impossible.

Liberated from the pressure to deliver bland, mass-market fare at high volume, more chefs are becoming business owners in their own right, earning a living producing high-quality, gourmet food at remarkably low prices. This innovation is shaking up the restaurant industry and inspiring efforts at protective regulation in cities all over the country.

The food trucks do present some regulatory challenges for local governments, but none of them are particularly difficult. A mobile kitchen requires a different approach to sanitation and fire inspection. Their potential to disrupt street traffic has to be considered. And ownership turnover can create sales-tax-collection headaches. Those problems can be, and are, addressed fairly easily in other places. Los Angeles has managed to maintain safety with some of the loosest rules for any major metro. Chicago has a tough set of food-truck regulations, but still allows more locations and greater concentration than Houston does, and doesn't include

Houston's absurd requirement that groups of food trucks downtown keep a fire marshal onsite.

At issue is whether one set of honest, hard-working small-business owners with capital invested in their brick-and-mortar restaurants should get protection by the city against another set of hard-working small-business owners armed with an innovative business plan. That's it. The rest of the arguments are noise.

This food fight includes no legitimate regulatory concerns. No one is trying to gain a competitive advantage from pollution, public harm, or some other moral hazard. What makes this regulatory fight unique is its unusual zero-sum character. Healthy competition normally does more than just re-slice the economic pie; it makes a bigger pie for everyone. However, in the food business, no matter how big the pie gets, you can only eat so much of it.

The restaurant owners are not just being short-sighted. Competition in this case is unlikely to lead to greater wealth for everyone in the picture. There are going to be some clear winners and losers from the City Council's decision. If the food trucks become a vibrant, permanent feature of Houston's food scene, creative chef-entrepreneurs, lovers of great food, and consumers in general will all likely benefit. On the other hand, it is reasonable to expect that some restaurant owners could lose their businesses.

More than that, many restaurant entrepreneurs will lose valuable leverage they once had over their chefs and staff. The food trucks open up freelance opportunities that disrupt the kitchen hierarchy. By slashing the capital requirements for starting a business, chefs no longer have to work through the system for decades in order to open their own enterprise. Anyone with a good head, a strong work ethic, and an appealing concept can take their work straight to the public on the strength of a modest investment.

Food trucks don't just threaten to change the dining room, they could change the kitchen. In the process, food trucks might be the test case for a wave of innovation that offers to transform many jobs we have traditionally thought of as blue-collar.

A little over a century ago, industrialization turned butchers from artisans into factory workers. A freshly dynamic economy is changing them back. Along the way, it is creating for them the strange and wonderful possibility of becoming a sort of minor celebrity in a formerly blue-collar niche.

Food-related businesses are leading the way, but we are seeing the emergence of this happy phenomenon around clothing design and production, construction, and many other forms of work that were very recently dominated by mass, industrial, hierarchical vendors.

The age of the steady job is definitely coming to a close, but it is being replaced by new, better opportunities that few people anticipated. Avoiding the urge to crush disruptive innovations through local protective regulations will be just one of the keys to maximizing the potential for former wage earners to become entrepreneurs.

The main Houston City Council meeting in 2013 to consider looser food-truck regulations was a circus. One councilman even mused about the threat of food-truck terrorism as he fumbled through the discussion. The absurdity of the debate reflected the Council's unwillingness to confront the core question involved. Its members hope that this will just go away. Their approach is, unfortunately, typical across the country.

The real test of a culture's strength is its capacity to tolerate disruptive change. America has become the world's great hub of technical advancement in large part because we do not allow existing institutions to harness government power in order to crush emerging competition. We recognize the moral and material value of creative destruction.

Local governments' stance on food-truck regulation may seem like a minor issue, but it is the small things that shape the large. Giving food-truck entrepreneurs a seat at the table offers everyone a slice of a better tasting future.

Why Is the Workforce Shrinking?

One of the most disturbing puzzles in the post-collapse economy is the rapid decline in workforce participation. Much of the improvement in the unemployment rate since 2009 has come from the large number of workers withdrawing from the labor pool. There is little agreement on what has caused the decline, but this may be a less important statistic than we generally believe. A wider look at workforce-participation rates may reveal that this decline is a product of a richer, more dynamic economy, rather than a result of the recession.

Economists generally clump around three potential explanations for declining workforce participation. All of them are certainly contributing to the numbers of the short term. A large cohort from the Baby Boomer generation is retiring, many people have abandoned the work force due to the inability to find work, and disabilities have surged.

Looking at these trends over the short term may be distorting our assessment of what's really happening. What these trends don't show is the larger set of structural forces that are going to drive down workforce participation further, even after the economy has fully recovered. The best clue for this comes from the long-term workforce participation in the most affluent segment of our population: white males.

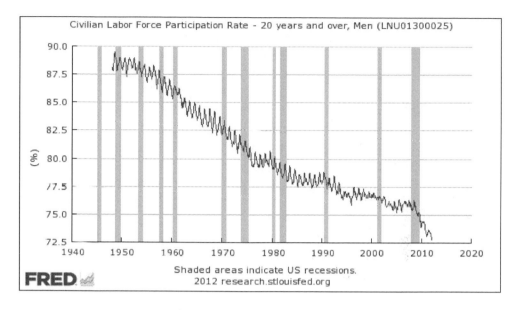

Civilian Labor Force Participation Rate - 20 years and over, Men (LNU01300025)

Shaded areas indicate US recessions.
2012 research.stlouisfed.org

FRED

Labor-force participation by adult white men has been on a continuous, steep decline since we started measuring it in the 1940s. That's not because white folks are so shiftless. It's because the country is getting steadily richer.

The length of a productive career, as a percentage of a lifetime, has been dropping steadily as capitalism advances. That process has accelerated dramatically since the rise of global capitalism a generation ago. Yes, fewer jobs are available at the low end of the economic spectrum than there were 50 years ago, but that's not the only dynamic at work.

A productive, successful career starts later and ends earlier than it ever has. The most-lucrative careers don't crank up until a worker is nearly 30, and they taper off to more or less voluntary work, or entrepreneurship, about 20 years later.

White males have been the first to experience this transformation because they have traditionally enjoyed the greatest access to the best careers, but this transformation is spreading through the rest of the culture. We are seeing a steeper shift right now because of an unusually weak economy and the beginning of the Baby Boomers' retirement cycle. However, declining workforce-participation rates are likely to continue even as the economy recovers.

More and more people spend years in higher education, when they are left off of the workforce statistics. Many more people interrupt a career midstream for advanced education. During transitions into entrepreneurship, many workers who formerly showed up as part of the workforce are temporarily off the ledger, sometimes for extended periods of time. Mothers and fathers, thanks to growing prosperity, find themselves in a position to take time away from their careers to raise children.

Likewise, as more women and minorities begin to get the same access to high-end careers that white males have enjoyed for generations, their career arc will resemble those of white males. Many of the most successful careers now include relatively lengthy stretches outside the official workforce during the 20–65 age range.

The single largest reason that more people, especially higher earners, are working shorter careers is because they can. That's why workforce participation by white men has been in steady decline for as long as those statistics have been kept. Understanding this dynamic changes the range of relevant policy approaches pretty dramatically.

The Cruel Myth of the Gateway Job

For conservatives, one of the central arguments against a minimum income or even a minimum wage is the notion that employment is a value in and of itself. Taking a low-paying job, no matter how menial or "dead-end," is supposed to be an exercise in character-building that places a person on the ladder of upward mobility. Therefore, anything that prevents someone from working is contributing to sloth and moral decay.

Perhaps it was true once. There really was a time in America when an unskilled, menial job could be a gateway to a rewarding career. But one of the reasons CEOs now earn hundreds of times more than their entry-level employees is that menial jobs have become a gateway to nowhere. In a knowledge economy, the on-ramp to post-middle-class affluence is located in a place fewer and fewer people can reach.

Research is starting to demonstrate the nature of the problem. A study performed by Bright.com found that people who perform low-wage, menial labor in service industries or work in fast food *at any point in their careers* tend to have depressed incomes throughout their lifetimes. If you ever work at Wendy's, you have roughly a 5% chance of someday earning at least $70,000 a year. Working at Ford, by contrast, suggests a 50% chance of eventually earning a median income. Lousy jobs are a gateway to other lousy jobs.

This matters because the myth of the gateway job is blocking policies that might open up greater access to opportunity and enable America to more productively develop our vast pool of human potential. Labor is not what it used to be. In a knowledge economy, labor is not strongly distinguished from capital. It can be developed, shaped, enhanced, and turned into more than a zero-sum resource. Labor, paired with a great deal of personal investment, can actually be used to accumulate enough capital to one day live on. This requires time, determination, and opportunity.

The logic behind the research on gateway jobs is relentless, and the pressure operates the same way whether you're looking at a bright young kid trying to work his way out of the ghetto or a college graduate. Dropping into menial labor has much the same results as dropping out of school, limiting the potential to develop labor as capital. Accessing and remaining on the ladder toward higher-earning careers requires the ability to support a long cycle of education and the economic freedom to make choices about what kinds of work to engage in.

We end up with too many people trying (and failing) to go to college because it is the only path for which we offer any subsidies. Among those who do attend college and develop crucial skills like effective communication and a spectacular capacity to learn, many graduates of non-technical colleges end up tracked too soon into work that offers little chance to put their skills to work.

Most of them eventually find their way because the skills and networks developed in the college environment give them most of what they need to succeed in a knowledge economy. They will tend to pick up additional skills on their own as needed, because ultimately that's what a degree in philosophy or medieval English poetry delivers. College graduates earn more than high-school graduates, even if they spent four years majoring in feminist literary studies, because they developed the skills that will allow them to continue to learn and adapt throughout their lifetime.

Pressure to move into full-time work is even more damaging for those who might want to pursue careers in fields that require skilled industrial labor. No one walks away from the grill at McDonald's one day to take their new job as an underwater welder or aircraft mechanic. Developing the ability to compete for those kinds of jobs is time-consuming and expensive. If you do not have a family that can support you while you learn and some time or exposure to discover that these careers even exist, these options are out of reach.

Employers cannot afford to pay a living wage while training a vast pool of potential recruits in key skills. Potential recruits with an interest in higher-skilled jobs cannot afford to prepare for those jobs if it requires them to forgo earning a living while taking out student loans for two or three years.

Someone who takes that job at Home Depot or Wendy's in order to support themselves is limiting their range of options for developing a more productive career. Front-line menial labor is supposed to create opportunities to climb the economic ladder, but it generally does not. More often than not, such jobs are a gateway to a lifetime of economic underachievement. A few employees in these positions might later look back on their experiences and suggest that the "lessons" learned from their early job became the key to their success. There may be a few elements of those experiences missing from the analysis.

Almost all of us beyond a certain age spent years doing menial work part-time, as an adjunct to something more important we were doing. Very few of us, if we have achieved much higher salaries in very successful careers, ever had to perform that work *in order to survive or feed a family.* If we did, whatever lessons we gained came at the cost of lost opportunities for higher-paying careers that we may not even be aware of.

There's a lot to learn from doing a menial job. Many of us can look back on poorly paid work that taught us crucial values. Or we could look back on years of training for an academic or athletic competition that did exactly the same thing without sucking time and energy out of a career path. We may press our kids to experience menial labor to help develop grit and a greater awareness of the world, but we will work hard to keep those experiences from becoming necessary for their survival.

Affluent white kids on the construction site or behind the store counter are usually tourists. They are attending a blue-collar summer camp. The "lessons" of that experience come at a high price for those workers who have to stay behind when the campers go back to their real work at Michigan State.

A shift away from the traditional safety net toward a form of minimum income offers a lot of benefits. One of the strongest criticisms of such a move, the fact that it would undermine the need to take menial work to survive, is actually one of its strengths. Pushing people too soon into menial work is as economically valuable as pushing 12-year-olds into a coal mine. A shift toward a minimum income would not only streamline our government, it would improve economic opportunity in almost exactly the same way that a universal public education once did.

Our attachment to the supposedly ennobling value of menial labor is dysfunctional and frankly condescending. Many of the same voices who crow about the value of work go to great lengths to prevent their kids from falling into its trap. We should not let a myth about gateway jobs prevent us from opening up broader economic opportunity and better developing American talent in a brutally competitive global market.

Why Not Use Unions?

Ask a Democrat what created the American middle class and many of them will answer: "unions." Organized labor gave factory workers badly needed leverage in negotiations with capital owners at a time when government refused to use its power to help them. Armed with that power, unions negotiated working terms and wages that made it possible for laborers to enjoy a decent standard of living.

Now, as the rapidly accelerating pace of technology and automation are eroding demand for lower-skill jobs and delivering higher and higher returns to a few, could workers benefit from a new push toward unionization? The answer is no, and that answer has serious implications for policy and politics.

The purpose of a union is to provide employees with the bargaining leverage they need to secure reasonable working conditions and compensation. This was particularly important in an industrial setting where human labor was little more than an extension of a factory's machines.

Each individual employee swinging a hammer was what economists call "fungible"—what he or she offered in value was indistinguishable from the value offered by the next person in line. There was very little about the labor being performed in most industrial-era settings that would encourage owners to compete for a specific employee. Workers were as replaceable as a pair of gloves.

Fungible labor set up a permanent downward bidding war in which employers had every incentive to set compensation and working conditions ever lower. By collaborating in unions, workers could apply pressure on capital owners to counter their bargaining weakness. In an atmosphere in which there was virtually no support from government to protect workers' rights and labor itself was entirely fungible, unions were the key to the creation of a decent way of life. For their time, unions were an innovation that helped ordinary people enjoy a greater share of the wealth generated by industrialization and created a decent life for millions of people.

Many people blame outsourcing and international competition for the decline of labor unions, but that claim misses the more-fundamental economic changes that brought those dynamics about. Two very important things have changed in our economy that have undermined the value of unions and converted them into a death sentence for businesses that must work with them.

First, the rise of state regulation of working conditions made the most important work of a union unnecessary. With a wage floor, safety regulations, workers compensation, universal public education, Social Security, and other state interventions, much of the value that unions were organized to deliver became redundant. Regulation was more attractive than unions in many ways because it imposed a uniform set of conditions on all employers, creating a scenario in which every firm competed on the same level field. In order to maintain their appeal to members, unions evolved into a general buffer between employees and management, adding dense layers of bureaucracy to even the most routine hiring, firing, and administrative decisions.

Add to that the second factor, the rise of automation and information-based competition, and you get a deadly cocktail. The rise of the knowledge economy and the sudden, dramatic expansion in the range of activities vulnerable to automation created a dynamic that killed off organizations bound by unions. If every change in work hours, labor force, or job description requires a new collective bargaining agreement, it will be impossible to keep pace with innovations that radically reduce manufacturing costs and introduce more-rapid adaptive capabilities.

Companies free from the straightjacket of a collective bargaining agreement can change more quickly, adopting leaner practices. No matter how well-managed, innovative, or responsible, competitors saddled with collective bargaining agreements drag behind, unable to lower their costs or develop new value fast enough to compete.

In some cases, work is shipped overseas, where labor is cheaper and less effectively organized, but we are discovering that this is merely an intermediate step in the decline of the low-skilled workforce. Firms like Nike are already laying off hundreds of thousands of contract workers in the developing world as the race toward higher efficiency and adaptability makes automation more attractive than even the cheapest labor. China-based Foxconn, manufacturer of the iPhone and one of the largest commercial employers in the world, is collaborating with Google on a long-term automation project that would eliminate hundreds of thousands of factory jobs.

Innovation, not outsourcing, is the root factor in the decline of manufacturing employment in the U.S. More restrictive laws and collective bargaining will not help. Market conditions are changing in ways that make low-skilled, undifferentiated labor inherently less valuable. Those same forces are opening up new opportunities for far more rewarding work, but gaining access to that work is more challenging. That condition is just as relevant in China as it is in Detroit.

The bulk of jobs that benefit most from unionization are simply disappearing. They aren't merely going overseas. They are going away.

The low-wage jobs that remain are mostly in service industries like fast food and retail. We could pressure those industries to unionize, but we would merely be repeating the dynamic that favored nonunion companies in manufacturing fields. The problem with unions is that they are too bureaucratic and slow to survive in a highly dynamic economy. Protecting information-age jobs and lifestyles with unions built to work under industrial conditions is like trying to hold water in your fists.

Force companies to adopt broader unionization, and we will further accelerate the move toward automation. Unions would offer nothing more than stagnation and mediocrity as a fleeting bulwark against the relentless tide of economic dynamism. If we are going to improve living conditions, opportunity, and rewards for those who do not make it into knowledge-based careers or entrepreneurship, we need an alternative to organized labor.

The Shape of the World

Our culture and economy have changed in a very short time frame, in ways that are discontinuous and in some cases dangerously disruptive. These changes came with little warning, and though they have been generally welcome, no one anticipated their implications. Not everyone is thrilled with the new shape of the world, and that dissatisfaction is roiling politics here at home as well as globally.

What has happened and where we are, in summary:

- We won the Cold War.

- The spread of market capitalism around the world has led to an explosive expansion of wealth and freedom at home and abroad.

- Few of us recognize the massive scope of this victory. We are more apt to see the frightening new challenges spun up by this radical change in circumstances than the amazing benefits it continues to bring.

- Sudden new freedom and wealth are causing surprising unintended consequences. Social-capital institutions, that network of local groups that has formed the foundation of our political system from the very beginning, are falling apart under the pressure of greater personal choice.

- Our world is changing at an accelerating pace, creating mental strain and fear.

- The collapse of social capital coupled with the disorienting impact of an accelerating pace of change is breeding weirdness in our politics. Paranoia is rising to the surface while more-considered voices are largely absent from the process.

- An economy of extremes is bringing wildly unequal outcomes while our social safety net and other economic buffers are not meeting the challenge.

- Capitalism is becoming a culture, steadily reducing everything to the sum of the value it can command in a market transaction.

- For those who are adapting successfully to this emerging environment, the "job" is becoming less central to our economy and our lives. Formal employment is being replaced by a wide range of options for earning a living. In many cases, this is making people rich. In too many cases, it is leaving masses of people behind without a reasonable hope of earning a living.

- This collection of forces is weakening every traditional center of authority, unleashing an unexpected devolution of power that threatens our core institutions.

Our political institutions have a critical role to play in helping us manage our transition to a world of accelerating, discontinuous change, but those institutions are struggling under challenges of their own. How do we restore some basic effectiveness to our politics?

Recognizing what we are experiencing is a fine start. The next step might require us to think a little harder about the meaning of our traditional political divide.

Everything we think we know about the meaning of left, right, and center is still based on assumptions shaped by the Cold War. Sitting beneath that outdated divide are a set of much older, much deeper ideas about our relationship to government, the meaning of "freedom," and our duties to each other.

Policies that will help us bridge this transition will not come from one party or the other, at least not the way they are currently configured. Our political parties are organized around policy disagreements that have, for the most part, become irrelevant. We need to better recognize the core issues obscured by partisan loyalties and begin forming policies that can rally a broad majority across traditional party lines. Doing that means looking past artificial political boundaries and meaningless team labels.

Part 2: Redefining Left, Right and Center in a Post–Cold War World

For 50 years, American politics was distorted by the pressure of living in a state of permanent semi-war. All of the country's traditional controversies were sublimated in the interest of national protection. The Cold War left us more centrally governed than we had ever been and our core conflicts had been warped almost beyond memory. Those old political orientations did not disappear; they merely lost their reference points.

Right and left, conservative and liberal, Republican and Democrat are terms we still use in political discourse, but their relationship to their heritage is almost completely lost. We redefined them on the basis of Cold War demands until we forgot what they meant. Now that we've emerged from that long conflict, one lingering controversy from our earliest roots is reasserting itself at the center of our politics.

As the country decisively abandons its rural heritage and the economic engine of our future moves deeper and deeper into our largest cities, we are being forced to reckon with a debate as old as the Republic. One political rivalry more than any other explains how we will frame our future.

Hamilton vs. Jefferson again, and again, and again ...

When General Lee handed Ulysses S. Grant his surrender and my ancestors went home in defeat, there was reason to believe that one of the great unresolved conflicts over the meaning of the American experiment had been laid to a bloody rest.

I'm not talking about slavery. The most important original argument over America's identity was best encapsulated in the competing visions of Thomas Jefferson and Alexander Hamilton. And the end of the Civil War did not in fact prove to be the end of that argument.

Simply put, Hamilton was a proto-capitalist New York banker who wanted to see the country embrace an economic and political model that prioritized commerce over agriculture. His vision would require a strong central government to invest in infrastructure and regulation. It demanded a powerful central authority to manage currency and banking. It favored cities over the countryside, industry over agriculture, capital over land.

Jefferson was a Southern plantation owner who wanted to build a slave republic dominated by landholders where each landowning citizen was practically sovereign on his own property. His model required almost no central government. It demanded weak governing authorities at every level. It prioritized individual liberty over justice, a model that offered unique appeal to an emerging class of small landholders while protecting the interests of a slaveholding aristocracy. It was simple in design, cheap to maintain, and in the beginning it was dominant, especially in the South.

In the years after the American Revolution, Northern states began a shift toward Hamiltonian capitalism. Over strenuous Southern objections, those states, and the federal government wherever possible, began chartering banks, building canals, expanding ports, and laying railroad tracks. You can't develop a coal industry in Pennsylvania if you can't ship the product to New York. Building that infrastructure would require more organization and capital than individuals or banks could fund on their own, but would yield massive benefits to a wide swath of the country.

Southerners fought to block most federal expenditures for infrastructure. President Jefferson himself dismissed the Erie Canal as "little short of madness." His fellow Virginian, President James Madison, vetoed an effort to fund it. It was eventually financed by New York State. It brought massive new wealth to the Great Lakes basin and solidified New York City as the economic center of the nation.

It brought nothing to the South.

My Southern ancestors lived quiet, rural lives. The harshest and most dangerous labor in their world was performed by slaves, giving them a sort of borrowed dignity regardless of whether they owned any slaves themselves. Religion was paramount, followed by family, clan, and country. Their agricultural model and warm climate left them free from the need to organize any meaningful government beyond basic police and courts.

There were trains and factories, but few of them. Southern states resisted any organized industrial planning and fought federal efforts to build infrastructure. Southerners feared that the rise of industrial capitalism and the infrastructure it demanded would destroy their massive investment in slavery and undermine the ethic of white supremacy that offered them such essential comfort and social unity. They were right.

Capitalism creates a gravity toward innovation, urbanization, education, and public infrastructure. The complexity that accompanies capitalism creates pressure on public institutions to expand. Capitalism assigns scarce resources based on open competition, a dynamic that threatens traditional institutions based on race and inheritance. It grants ever increasing power to those who wield disruptive innovation to challenge old ways of operating. It gradually shifts power toward an aristocracy of initiative and intellect, weakening power based on family, religion, and tradition.

Capitalism is as hostile to white supremacy as it is to charity, compassion, or conservation. Jeffersonians opposed its spread through every possible means. As a consequence, when the Civil War came, the South never had a chance. Having missed the Industrial Revolution almost entirely, the Confederacy was weaker than the Northern states in almost every respect. The Jeffersonian model didn't just leave them trailing in factories and railroads. As former Senator James Webb pointed out in his book *Born Fighting*:

"With only one-third of the white population, the south had nearly two thirds of its richest men and a large proportion of the very poor ... In 1860 seven eighths of [foreign] immigrants came to the north ... In the north, 94% of the population was found to be literate by the census of 1860; in the south barely 54% percent could read and write. Roughly 72% of northern children were enrolled in school compared with 35% of the same age in the south."

Southerners' martial spirit made them formidable fighters, but they were lousy at coordination and unable to match the North's infrastructure advantages. The Confederacy with its Jeffersonian economy was plowed under by the massive organizational power of a capitalist civilization. It lost because it had built a weaker, poorer system.

Wars don't necessarily change cultures. The South has experienced waves of Federal Reconstruction, including the postwar occupation, the New Deal, and the civil-rights movement. Yet my people have never openly confronted the central question that still hangs in the air.

In the southern states in the early 21st century, politicians almost universally speak favorably of capitalism, but only because they have lost any sense of what the term means. Southern conservatives are as steeped in Jeffersonian values as they have ever been. The term *capitalism* as wielded by southern conservatives today means simply "not socialism." It is the opposite of anything that smacks of activist government. Conservatives in the South remain as hostile to Hamiltonian commercial capitalism as my ancestors were.

No one can say out loud that they are fighting for the Confederate way of life, and some who embrace it may not even recognize it. You can get some hints at what's going on if you probe Ron Paul's fans for their thoughts on Lincoln. The weird AM-radio and Tea Party rhetoric of fighting "socialism" sounds absurd, but only if you take the term literally. As a proxy for the neo-Confederate economic and cultural model, this language makes perfect sense.

The fight against socialism is over, and capitalism is now virtually unchallenged as the global economic model. Socialism is as relevant to American politics as is monarchy. Despite the noisy rhetoric, policy debate in America no longer has any relationship to that dead conflict. Though few of us recognize it, Americans in our era have gone back to fighting over our most fundamental ideological conflict, older than either capitalism or communism. It's still about Jefferson and Hamilton.

Hamilton's model has always been more practical, more prosperous, more powerful, and unfortunately far less romantically appealing than Jefferson's. The emergence of a muscular new global capitalism over the past generation has shifted the balance of power decisively away from Jefferson. The dominant ethics of Jefferson's slave republic are so grotesquely out of place that they can no longer be defended directly.

It's no longer a fair competition. In our era, Jeffersonian democracy is a prescription for poverty, injustice, oppression, and ultimately economic decline. Perhaps it always was. Cultures that prosper in the 21st century will be the ones that master the organizational challenges to building the infrastructure that capitalism demands. At the same time, they will have to master the other great challenge of the age: balancing the growing demand for organization with the need to preserve individual liberty and innovation.

This may be the era of Hamilton's triumph, but Jefferson's legacy of concern for the individual beyond the commercial realm may be the lingering, vestigial X factor that will give Americans their edge. As we ready ourselves for new challenges, we may find that it's all about Hamilton and Jefferson again, and again, and again.

Less Government, Less Freedom?

There's a lot of talk, particularly among Republicans, about rising threats to our freedom. Their concern is legitimate, but tragically misdirected. It's true that the accelerating complexity of our lives is bringing intrusions that we never anticipated. However, in the pursuit of a certain notion of freedom, conservatives are closing off avenues of personal choice that are crucial to leading a dignified and reasonably prosperous existence.

It is time to settle once and for all one gnawing element of the Jefferson vs. Hamilton controversy: Less government does not always produce more freedom.
Our fetish for a certain brand of freedom is destroying the broader ability of many Americans to make vitally important decisions for themselves. If we are going to build an authentic, relevant liberty accessible to everyone in a dynamic, urban society, we need to think a little harder about what freedom really means.

The freest man on Earth is the guy who has just been dropped off alone on a tiny deserted island. No government can force him to register a weapon. No tax collector will cull his earnings. He won't even have his evenings disrupted by unwanted sales calls that impinge on his privacy. No state or man will dictate his choices. Freedom. Sweet freedom.

And he'll be dead in just a few days. In the face of absolute *freedom*, he is left with a deeply constrained collection of *choices*. His former neighbors living under the oppressive, tax-hungry government of California may choose to sit down with a beer this evening and binge-watch *House of Cards* on Netflix. He will not have access to that choice. He will struggle to open a coconut in the hope that it might slake his thirst. His benighted friend who slaves under the oppression of

Obamacare back in Los Angeles visits a doctor to have an unsightly mole removed. Meanwhile the wounds he got when he tripped over vines fester and turn. Freedom isn't free.

"Freedom" that fails to open up new and better choices is not freedom at all. Human beings survive only in cultures. Our pursuit of freedom is never absolute. At every stage of human development, we surrendered a limited range of personal choices in exchange, hopefully, for better choices. The better choices ensured our survival while also giving us access to greater personal liberty.

We still engage in this compromise. Sometimes we do this in market transactions, like when we agree to perform work for an employer in exchange for money. Sometimes we make this compromise collectively through our political system, like when we agree to impose safe working conditions on employers through government action.

Only one of those compromises of my personal freedom is made in the free market, but both of those compromises expand my liberty by giving me a broader, better range of potential choices. Both of those compromises have the effect of expanding liberty. That's the crucial element of the balance of state power that Republicans seem to have completely abandoned.

Government is not the only force that can limit my freedom. In many cases, only through government action can I guarantee the maximum of personal liberty. That's why we impose taxes to maintain, for example, a military, courts, and a police force. That's why we are subject to jury duty. If you listen to a contemporary Republican talk about government, you're left to wonder whether there is any crucial function they would not dismantle.

This does not mean that more government delivers more choice. It means that the two factors do not operate as a zero-sum trade-off in the real world. There are very large, relatively intrusive governments in Western Europe, for example, that give their citizens a remarkably broad range of personal choices. Needless to say, there are also some very large, intrusive governments that do not. And there are large ungoverned swaths of Latin America and Africa where freedom is an utterly alien concept.

We gain nothing when we shrink government for the sake of shrinking government. The challenge of the post–Cold War period is to adapt government institutions to operate effectively in an atmosphere of accelerating economic and cultural dynamism. The kind of highly bureaucratic, "expert" government that was the hallmark of the Western democracies in the 20th century is becoming too bulky and unresponsive to survive.

Should we have more government or less government? The question is meaningless without context. Is $250,000 too much to pay for a house? It is impossible to answer that question intelligently without considering more variables.

We need to find a way to deliver the most crucial function of government—expanding overall access to the best possible range of choices–while we also shift toward a governing structure that is lighter, smarter, and more adaptable. In most cases, that prerogative dictates a smaller government, at least in terms of the size of the bureaucracy. However, it may also mean that government evolves to perform many functions it has not performed in the past.

The question is not more government versus less. Our goal is better government. Going forward, our purpose for government should not be to protect us from every harm or resolve every personal problem. The purpose of government should be to create a broader template for individual choices. That mission, not some blind, generalized hostility to government, should dictate the shape of public policy.

Complexity Demands Nimble Government

We need the organizing power of a strong central government to help us deliver the infrastructure and safety net essential to the survival of capitalism, but that doesn't mean that we can continue as we have with the near endless expansion of federal power and bureaucracy. Twentieth-century "big government" was marked by dense, professional bureaucracies that were slow to change but guaranteed job security and provided increasing independence from political control and accountability.

This trend cannot continue. Our accelerating economic and cultural transformation has outstripped the capacity of our political system to keep pace. The strong regulatory state, which attempts to write new rules to manage each new development in the marketplace, is utterly overmatched.

Our government is unreasonably expensive and slow because we have not yet adjusted our expectations. We need government more than ever, but it must find a way to deliver public services with a lighter, more humble hand. This not merely a preference. It will be the difference between effectiveness and irrelevance.

Perhaps the best place to see the limits of 20th-century bureaucratic government is with a close look at the Affordable Care Act. The Act itself (not including the virtually endless body of regulations that will continue to spew from it) is 2,409 pages of largely technical language. It's the equivalent of about two and half Bibles consisting only of the "Jehasephat begat Flimflameram" passages. Most of it reads like this:

"(1) GENERAL COST-SHARING LIMITATIONS.—Section 1916 of the Social Security Act (42 U.S.C. 10 13960) is amended in each of subsections (a)(2)(B) and (b)(2)(B) by inserting ', and counseling and pharmacotherapy for cessation of tobacco use by pregnant women (as defined in section 1905(bb)) and covered outpatient drugs (as defined in subsection (k)(2) of section 1927 and including

nonprescription drugs described in subsection (d)(2) of such section)' ..."

The fact that I don't understand the text of the law does not reflect on its merits. However, the fact that so few of the men and women who voted on the ACA know what it says raises troubling questions about our political process.

Friedrich Hayek anticipated this problem. He wrote *The Road to Serfdom* in Britain during World War II in response to growing calls for political and economic centralization. Hayek explained that intrusive efforts to control economic activity, no matter how well intentioned or popular, would be stymied by complexity:

"It would be impossible for any mind to comprehend the infinite variety of different needs of different people which compete for the available resources and to attach a definite weight to each."

We might all agree that we want a certain highly detailed and complex government program enacted, but a truly responsive political system would be pulled in a million directions as it confronted each of the elements of the program's execution. An originally clear mandate would disintegrate into a muddle as the vast spectrum of conflicting interests each get their say:

"The inability of democratic assemblies to carry out what seems to be a clear mandate of the people will inevitably cause dissatisfaction with democratic institutions. Parliaments come to be regarded as ineffective 'talking shops', unable or incompetent to carry out the tasks for which they have been chosen. The conviction grows that if effective planning is to be done, the direction must be 'taken out of politics' and placed in the hands of experts, permanent officials or independent autonomous bodies."

In Hayek's view, the public desire for increasing government planning ultimately threatens democratic legitimacy. He was right, and we are seeing the effects all around us.

It is vital to remember that Hayek, for all his concern about runaway centralization, was a realist when it came to the role of the state. He embraced laws to manage externalities and improve the lives of the less fortunate. He supported pollution controls, a minimum wage, and workplace-safety mandates. He acknowledged that government isn't the only potential source of oppression and that government action is necessary to maintain a free market.

He explained that competition requires the "adequate organization of certain institutions like money, markets, and channels of information—some of which can never be adequately provided by private enterprise." However, Hayek argued that when government attempts to solve the most-complex, individualized human problems through detailed, expert planning, human liberty gets crushed in the wheels of progress.

As a nation becomes more diverse, wealthy, representative, and populous, the ability of the central state to effectively regulate private activities in detail declines. Denmark has a population slightly larger than metropolitan Houston. Its citizens overwhelmingly share the same language, cultural heritage, and deeply intertwined social institutions. The Danish public sector accounts for almost 60% of the country's GDP (compared with less than 20% in the U.S.).

The Danes can, to an extent, support a big government. Their small population is deeply interconnected through robust institutions of social capital that incorporate their will into public decision making. As deeply as far governing institutions may intrude into the marketplace, their government still is not all that big in raw institutional terms.

America is not Denmark. Our federal government has to account for the needs of more than 300 million people spread across a continental land mass spanning seven time zones and reaching from the Arctic to the tropics. Our citizenry represents a global microcosm of cultural, religious, economic, and regional interests. We cannot make expert government work while preserving the personal liberty we treasure. Federal authority could operate differently and still protect the public from pollution, monopoly, and abuse by the powerful, but neither party seems sincerely interested in exploring ways to do this.

Democrats long for panels of smart people to shape our world, picking our energy sources, industrial policies, educational priorities, groceries—making all of the choices that we as citizens are too stupid to make for ourselves. The present crop of Republicans would, if turned loose, tear down nearly every barrier that protects ordinary people from abuse while building a government that would follow you all the way home, up the stairs, and into your bedroom.

Government has plenty of room to operate between these two poles if we demand it, but how? What would regulation look like if it were constrained by a greater sensitivity to federal overreach? What if it were possible to have a smarter, more effective government that still met all our basic needs with a fraction of the bureaucracy and intrusion?

The problem with big government is that it cannot be sufficiently nimble to operate in an increasingly dynamic atmosphere. It is not possible to minutely govern the affairs of 300 million people spread across seven time zones without restraining their liberty to an intolerable degree. If the federal civil service were a city, it would be our fourth-largest. And it still isn't enough to get the job done by present methods.

We need to explore ways to change the mission and methods of government to meet modern needs while maintaining accountability and a capacity for change. It is possible to meet public needs with a more modest approach to federal power. Accomplishing this goal without destroying the basic protections we depend on will require us to look at problems with a new eye, scrambling the traditional left-right divide and replacing it with a focus on pragmatism.

Our Most Overregulated, Under-Regulated Industry

"The proposal of any new law or regulation of commerce which comes from merchants and manufacturers should always be listened to with great precaution, and ought never to be adopted till after having been long and carefully examined with the most suspicious attention."
— Adam Smith, *The Wealth of Nations*

The Securities Act of 1933 is one of the most elegant and successful pieces of complex legislation in history. In less than 60 pages, it constructed a regulatory framework that would allow Wall Street to survive its self-immolation and reemerge as the engine of Western capitalism.

The Dodd-Frank Act, on the other hand, is a lumbering, 2,300-page behemoth of special-interest carve-outs. Dodd-Frank replaces 80 years of careful emphasis on informed risk with a smothering muddle of pointless new agencies and arcane rules.

Finance is probably the most overregulated, under-regulated sector of the economy. Washington's obsession with control has saddled the industry with appalling compliance costs while leaving the public increasingly exposed to abuse. There is no better way to illustrate this problem and its solution than to compare Dodd-Frank with the 1933 Securities Act.

Dodd-Frank adds to the current regulatory scheme three brand-new regulatory bodies and will require thousands of additional pages of enabling regulation. Why all the new agencies? Because in spite of its spectacular length, *the law did not actually update our regulatory scheme.* Congress delegated the hardest questions to the agencies.

Remember the second quote from Hayek cited above? Dodd-Frank does exactly what Hayek warned, taking almost the entire realm of financial regulation "out of politics" and placing it in the hands of unelected, unaccountable bureaucratic "experts." For many of those experts, their greatest personal goal is to cash out of their dull government jobs and move over to Wall Street. The banks utterly control their own regulators.

Dodd-Frank almost miraculously fails to halt the risky practices by federally insured banks and regulated entities that gave rise to the 2008 collapse. The Act does, however, seek to regulate the trade in blood diamonds, report on mine safety, and monitor minority hiring.

Dodd-Frank doesn't get federally insured banks out of the business of derivatives trading. It doesn't impose collateral or reserve requirements on banks or insurance companies trading collateralized debt obligations, or CDOs. The proprietary trading, mass securitization, and collusion between investment banks and rating agencies—it's all untouched. More than two thousand pages later, these matters are left to the regulators to sort out.

By contrast, why was the Securities Act of 1933 successful in building a reasonable regulatory foundation that successfully constrained fraud? Congress in 1933 resisted the urge to eliminate every market risk or anticipate every potential securities scenario.

Instead of trying to keep up with financial innovation, the Securities Act of 1933 created a regulated zone and required companies to abide by certain rules if they wished to access that zone. It did not try to keep qualitatively bad investments from reaching the public markets. It tried to keep *fraudulent* investments from reaching the public markets. The rules

101

emphasized disclosure and let investors judge quality on their own. Further, the Act preserved a range of innovation outside the regulated markets. There, investors could take greater risks, free from the burden of most regulation.

We've been slowly dismantling our regulatory structure since the Reagan years, but the effort has strangely increased the burden of financial regulation. To preserve federal protection over insurance and banking entities while allowing them to step outside this zone of protection, government has tried to keep pace with the accelerating rise in financial complexity. Government is inherently slow. It has not kept up.

We are left with a growing body of increasingly unstable banks, investment houses, and insurance companies. They find life under "deregulation" to be accompanied by an absurd burden of new and largely pointless documentation requirements as government struggles to keep pace with their innovations. Banks are doing more with your money than they were ever allowed to do before, and your government has little authentic grasp of their activities.

The philosophy behind the Depression-era financial regulations offers a template for a solution. Government should not try to protect what it can't comprehend. Federally protected entities like FDIC-insured banks should not engage in risky derivatives trading. Pension funds, 401(k) investors, most insurance companies, and other protected entities should not be allowed into commodities markets, derivatives, or other environments with a high disaster quotient.

Federally guaranteed organizations simply cannot be on the bleeding edge of financial innovation without dragging the public into their disasters. If regulated exchanges, insured banks, insurance companies, and our quasi-governmental mortgage financiers were constrained from dealing in exotic instruments engineered to obscure risks, we would never have been introduced to the phrase *too big to fail*. On the other hand, private-equity groups and hedge funds should be free to take on as much risk as they want within the limits of fraud laws.

Ambitious regulatory schemes like Dodd-Frank exist to protect financial institutions, allowing them to benefit from public backing while in engaging in activities for which they are not suited. The same problem haunts regulatory efforts in other fields like oil exploration, food safety, and education.

Effective regulation recognizes that government cannot do everything. It creates protected zones emphasizing transparency, while carefully limiting its own reach. Regulations that respect the public interest over special interests consistently do less and accomplish more.

Health Care Is Not a Market

"Where it is impossible to create the conditions necessary to make competition effective, we should resort to other methods of guiding economic activity."
—Friedrich Hayek, *The Road to Serfdom*

Here's a simple solution to our health-care mess: Eliminate all the insurance companies, government subsidies, and other intermediaries and let people purchase medical services directly from a provider of their choice at the going market rate.

Believe it or not, this is actually a popular concept on the Republican far right, and not just from Ron Paul. Call it the "chicken plan," after Republican Senator Tom Coburn's nostalgic comments on how well this program worked in the old days, when people bartered livestock for medical care.

Republicans still struggle to promote a credible ownership culture largely because they refuse to wrestle honestly with the hard cases, the situations in which market forces fail to allocate value effectively. Medical care is probably the most frustrating example because it stubbornly resists market solutions and affects everyone deeply.

Health care is not a market. It lacks any of the vital features of a market. Treating health care like a market means living (and dying) without modern medicine. To advance ownership culture, we need an alternative to state-controlled health care that keeps key decisions in personal hands, preserves market triggers where appropriate, and rids us of the strangling influence of the massive federal bureaucracy. Republicans cannot do this until they abandon some cherished fantasies about the unquestionable, divinely ordained righteousness of markets.

In a free market, goods and services are allocated through transactions entered into with mutual consent. No one is forced to buy from a particular supplier. No one is forced to engage in any transaction at all. If a price cannot be agreed on, then the transaction simply does not occur.

The medical industry exists to serve people who have been rendered incapable of representing their own interests in an adversarial transaction. When I need health services, I often need them in a way that is quite different from my desire for a good-quality television or a fine automobile. As I lay unconscious under a bus, I am in no position to shop for the best provider of ambulance services at the most reasonable price. All personal volition is lost. Whatever happens next, it will not be a market transaction.

Insurance is the obvious solution, but an insurance-funded medical system means abandoning an unregulated free market for health care. The insurer model creates a three-party managed market in which the patient has surrendered their buying power and much of their discretion to an entity whose interests are not aligned with their own. This arrangement can actually work quite well, but not under unregulated, free-market conditions.

We cannot maintain an insurance-based system of health care unless there is some force aligned with the consumer that has the superior authority and financial backing to hold the insurance providers to their end of the deal. What if my insurance company refuses to pay? What if the insurance company with which I contracted collapses and cannot pay for my medical care when I need it?

Patients, at the moment they purchase insurance, have no way to be certain which provider will actually deliver on its promise. They will only discover the answer when their life, or the lives of their family members, depends on it. Under an insurance system without regulation, the market forces that would exist in a face-to-face transaction between consumer (patient) and supplier (doctor) disappear, replaced with a grim gamble in which the provider has every incentive to cheat.

Modern health care with all its fancy instruments, amazing methods, and success in extending life and happiness exists only because we started abandoning the free market in medicine a century ago. Go back to paying your doctor with chickens and your doctor will go back to being a part-timer who learned his craft from a book in order to augment his income from farming. For those who love the creative power of capitalism, health care is a brutal frustration. Absent some framework created by a government, there is no market for health care.

Does that mean we will eventually have to submit to single-payer health care controlled entirely by the federal government? No, the developed world includes a kaleidoscope of different approaches to health care, from single-payer to almost exclusively private-insured, that deliver better care at lower cost than ours does. Alternatives to our current system exist, but so far conservatives have refused to even look at them.

It should be noted that until Obama got elected, the most popular health-care proposal among conservatives was the

Heritage Foundation's plan for an insurance mandate, formulated in 1989. Republicans in Congress proposed an individual mandate in 1993 as the Nickles-Stearns Bill, and it was supported by such notorious "RINOs" as Jesse Helms and Trent Lott. That plan was adopted by Massachusetts under Mitt Romney and eventually formed the core of the Affordable Care Act. It is hard to imagine any Republican now who could survive politically while dealing so honestly with health-care issues.

The biggest long-term structural obstacle to the progress of the ownership culture is our health-care system. It punishes entrepreneurs, chains employees to traditional work, and leaves millions of Americans without access to care. We count on conservatives to deliver pragmatic, sensible solutions, but when it comes to health care, Republicans are off their meds. Until Republicans are ready to move past their fundamentalist free-market fantasies, the spread of the ownership society will remain stalled.

The Purpose of the Social Safety Net

When my father was young, my grandfather was seriously injured in a ranch accident. He was unable to work for an extended time and was never able to return to his previous job. While he struggled to recover and find a new way to earn a living, a wife and four young children were left with very little support. The neighbors banded together to help, but their resources were limited.

The situation got steadily worse. A neighbor in town had a disused chicken coop with a standpipe for running water, and for a time that became the family's home. People occasionally brought food and helped out where they could.

The family survived, deeply hungry and cold, thanks to their own hardscrabble efforts and the mercies of the community around them. However, the damage in personal terms and in their future economic capacity was serious and sustained. The

Panhandle winter they passed in a renovated chicken coop would echo in a thousand little ways and across generations.

I was a young teenager when my father was crushed by a forklift in his third major industrial injury. He lived, but he was unable to work for more than a year and unable to ever return to his previous duties. Neighbors were supportive, but their efforts do not explain why we retained our home, our security, and our dignity. This difficult incident did not destroy our family financially because a few things had changed since the Chicken-Coop Winter.

Texas's evolving workers' compensation laws meant that Dad, unlike my grandfather, retained some income and access to health care while he recovered. We never needed welfare or food stamps because the middle-class portions of the safety net worked for us. Our educations were not interrupted. As kids we hardly noticed a change apart from Dad being around a lot more. We retained the same landscape of options for our lives that we had before the accident.

Those contrasting stories demonstrate what effective social programs are meant to accomplish. In the conservative vision, best expressed by the late Jack Kemp, the primary purpose of the safety net is not to eliminate poverty, mandate better decisions, or create some utopia in which all human suffering disappears. We maintain government assistance programs in order to *broaden the landscape of available choices.*

Republicans should take a breath, brace themselves, and repeat this sentence three times without puking: "Social-welfare programs can have positive effects."
An improved workers' compensation program gave my father a better range of choices than his father faced in the same situation. Those programs did not replace our individual responsibilities. They did not turn my family into "slaves to government." They freed us to pursue our potential.

How Republicans managed in such a short time to travel from Jack Kemp's enterprise zones and tenant ownership programs to Mitt Romney's "47%" slander is a sad story of fear-based politics and neo-Confederate nightmares. However, nothing keeps the party from retracing its steps and recapturing that positive vision.

On issues as varied as public schools and tax policy, there is a massive political gap waiting to be exploited by a party willing to embrace a pragmatic, bottom-up approach to social welfare. Progressives still promote government intervention that effectively replaces individual initiative with the guidance of elite experts. Their top-down, intrusive solutions embrace what George W. Bush once called "the soft bigotry of low expectations" and feeds endless bureaucratic expansion.

On the other hand, far-right conservatives consider nearly everything government does to be "socialism." The Dixiecratic refugees that fled into the Republican Party will wreck the safety net if they get half a chance.

A growing consensus believes that neither extreme has it right. There is room in that emerging consensus for conservatives to choose a fresh approach.

Poverty is influenced by personal decisions, but not everyone has access to the same choices. One person may have to decide whether she's willing work hard in school so that she'll be prepared to take over the family business from Dad. Another person may have to decide whether to resist the local gang that wants him to sell drugs.

Social welfare helps most when it expands, rather than replaces, personal options. Our safety net works best when we use public schools, welfare, food stamps, workers' compensation, unemployment, a progressive income tax, and a hundred other public-policy tools not to force people to make choices we find preferable, but to provide a better range of choices.

That doesn't mean every program will be geared to produce an entrepreneur. To be effective we have to acknowledge that the mentally ill, the addicted, the sick or elderly, those scarred by long years of abuse, and others may never take advantage of freer social mobility. Opening up the pathways of capital accumulation will not help them *directly*. Everyone should be offered the potential to stand on their own, but some among us will not master the skills to function effectively. We should cooperate through government to provide for their survival and protect their basic human dignity.

The social safety net is a form of personal-decision insurance. By cooperating through a representative government, we are preserving our access to certain choices that could otherwise be yanked away by fate.

The New Deal fight has been over for decades because it was a massive success. Conservatives need to get over it and play a role in shaping the future.

So Now What?

Once we come to recognize how the recent, continuing, and accelerating transformation of our culture and economy is creating unprecedented new strains on our governing institutions, what are we supposed to do about it?

We first have to recognize what we are experiencing. Out of that recognition can emerge potential political options that can serve as a rallying point for new majorities. Neither political party is offering a policy agenda that makes sense in light of post–Cold War concerns. The two parties are wrestling with each other to solve the problems of the '80s. The first major cohort in either existing party, or across both them, that steps forward with a realistic modern governing agenda can expect to dominate our politics for a generation or more.

Policy will have to come first, and that's both difficult and unusual. Traditionally, politics is dominated by organizations, not policy—hence the old adage that "All politics is local." But, as explained previously, the social-capital environment from which that adage sprang is dying. Politics at the block level is deeply ill where it still exists at all. The most powerful expression of grassroots politics in our era is the Tea Party movement. That's the quality of policy and engagement that emerges from traditional grassroots organizing now.

The next great wave of useful political energy likely will not come from the precincts. Through emerging new networks of social interaction, a consensus will have to emerge on a set of policy goals. Those goals will be the pole around which a new majority will form.

A sane, rational, public-interested majority is out there. For the most part they are busy managing their personal affairs. To the extent that they follow politics, they find it distasteful, seedy, and at times downright disgusting. Many would probably participate if offered promising options, but neither party is offering any such incentive at the moment. Both parties are held captive by their respective ideological cores, which are still arguing over the ghosts of yesterday's problems.

Assemble a set of rational policies, ambitious enough to matter and practical enough to work, and watch what happens.

The proposals that follow here are not perhaps the ones we need. No one person can design a policy agenda to take us forward. These ideas are meant to be the germ of a conversation, a starting point. Hopefully they touch on many, if not most, of the critical questions we need to answer in order to form a coherent new agenda.

Part 3: Policy Templates

The Republican Party's Best Idea

In the post–Cold War era, the rivalry between capitalism and socialism is over. There is no longer any credible political force advocating for government ownership of our major industries, guaranteed economic outcomes, central planning, mandatory union membership, and confiscatory taxes on high earners.

Our challenge now is to build an economic order that maximizes the wealth-generating power of markets while preserving a social safety net, protecting shared resources, and maximizing the opportunity for everyone to compete. For a brief period in the '90s, the Republican Party began to develop a very promising approach to this challenge. That effort crumbled for a variety of reasons, but the ownership society could, if properly refined and adapted, still become the core of a new majority and the launchpad for a new American Century.

The overriding ethic of the ownership society is that as many decisions as possible should be placed in individual hands. Making that work sometimes requires more government involvement that we are used to, but in most cases it involves less.

More important, this means that government shifts from being a decision-making force to being an infrastructure provider. Government doesn't decide which insurance plan you will have, for example; it builds and delivers the framework within which you make that choice for yourself.

This is important because it places less pressure on government to adapt to every potential market contingency, a burden it simply can no longer meet under the dynamic conditions of market capitalism. It means that government would be positioned to deliver an even larger range of public services with a smaller, more flexible bureaucracy. Smarter, leaner, more sustainable government might actually deliver more for the public than the 20ᵗʰ-century big-government behemoth.

An ownership society does not mean that government disappears from our lives. It means that government takes its rightful place in a market economy, ensuring that everyone has access to more, rather than fewer, options in life. The ownership society is less a specific policy than a political posture. In its first iteration, it was strangled by ideological demands that forbade Republicans from even acknowledging, much less addressing, some of the weaknesses in the concept. Nonetheless it remains a potent idea, the one most relevant to the needs of our time.

The ownership society is a world in which individuals have primary control over every aspect of their lives. Instead of a society that turns to government to deliver all of the basic requirements of life, government in the ownership society is merely an aid to a population in control of its own fate. Capital ownership is not limited to a wealthy elite, but is a standard feature of life for most people. Holding a full-time job provided to you by an institution or capital owner is only one of many different ways for middle-wealth families to earn a living.

Government in the ownership society is an enabler instead of a provider. It plays a key role in delivering infrastructure and a safety net, and enforcing the rules of the economic game, but it has little to do with economic outcomes. Unions are antiquated, because workplace protections are delivered by regulation. A vibrant technical and employment environment makes "job security" more of a shackle than a value.

The safety net in the ownership society is designed to be more of a trampoline and less of a spider web. It would actually be bigger, stronger, and reach more people than our current one does, but its emphasis would be vastly different.

Transforming the ownership society from political slogan to everyday reality would require Republicans to think hard about problems whose existence we mostly refuse to acknowledge. This approach to our culture has the potential to create devastatingly serious problems if hijacked by market fundamentalists.

Particularly in matters of health care, education, and regulation, laissez-faire policies would smother the ownership society in its crib. A culture of mass capital ownership will not emerge from economic anarchy. Failure to mitigate the negative impacts of this transition risks building a vast underclass, cut off from the opportunity to compete. Under a weak government, an ownership culture would quickly dissolve into a banana republic, making everyone poorer and less secure.

To make this transition work, we will have to focus on some ideologically uncomfortable problems and pragmatic solutions. How will minority groups and others with little current access to capital make the transition? How do we reduce the bureaucratic burdens on our capital markets without unleashing mass fraud—again? How do we bring about this transition without concentrating too much power in too few hands? How do we deal with problems that resist market solutions, like health care and environmental protection?

How do we square an emphasis on individual decision making with a respect for traditional values? What does an ownership culture mean for gay marriage, abortion, school prayer, and other social questions? Can social conservatism become the force that gives the ownership society its compassionate conscience?

The next American Century is a mass of tools and materials strewn all over our collective garage floor. It is available to us, but isn't going to build itself. We have to do some thinking and create a plan on which we can build a party and a culture for the future.

How to Win the War on Drugs

America passed a little-noted milestone in 2009, as drug overdoses outnumbered traffic fatalities for the first time ever to become the primary cause of accidental death. The main culprit? It wasn't cocaine or heroin or some terrifying new criminal import. Drug-related deaths doubled over the past decade in large part because of prescription-drug use.

We spend billions of dollars each year on a campaign to limit access to illegal narcotics, but we remain a heavily medicated society. Antidepressants alone are consumed on such a spectacular scale, they are starting to be found in significant concentrations in river fish.

The time has come for us to finally turn the tide in the drug war by imposing realistic access regulations and abandoning our policy of absolute prohibition. It won't happen overnight, but we need to start taking sensible steps toward narcotics regulation, starting with marijuana. Perhaps we could then turn our attention to the wider crisis of substance abuse.

Public enthusiasm for drug prohibition, especially as it relates to marijuana, is steadily eroding. State and local governments are looking for ways to make marijuana medically available and even rolling back enforcement aimed at recreational users. No presidential nominee from either party since the '90s could claim that he'd never smoked pot, and George W. Bush even waffled on the subject of cocaine use. Marijuana has become far too pervasive for draconian prohibition to make sense.

State and local governments' piecemeal efforts to ease marijuana prohibition can only create a muddle so long as federal prohibition remains in place. Representatives Ron Paul and Barney Frank, the oddest of odd couples, introduced legislation in 2011 that would have ended the federal prohibition on marijuana by simply removing the drug from the schedule of controlled substances. The legislation went nowhere. The public isn't ready to treat marijuana as if it were basil. It is still a powerful narcotic deserving of reasonable controls.

Colorado has been a remarkably successful test case for legalization so far, but problems exist. With no oversight on how the narcotic is blended into foods and drinks, children are gaining access to drugs that look like candy. Users unfamiliar with marijuana are being exposed to very high doses without understanding the implications. Decriminalization is a good idea. Complete deregulation is not.

Voters are ready for a considered effort to change the way we handle illicit drugs. The most significant barrier to public support for a reasonable drug-regulation scheme is the absence of any common-sense federal proposal.

What if users could purchase marijuana the way they buy tequila? Government would regulate the form, dosage, and delivery in much the same manner that we regulate other food and drugs. It could only be sold in limited volumes to a verified adult, in a form that meets quality and labeling standards.

What if farmers could be licensed to grow marijuana and sell it through a regulated channel? What if licensed adults could grow small quantities for their own use in the same way that people make their own beer or wine? What impact would such a change have on the local dealers scattered throughout America? (Hint: How many black-market beer dealers are there in your neighborhood?)

Getting from strict prohibition to regulation could be accomplished fairly quickly, and the public is ready to support it. Congress would have to amend the Controlled Substances Act, probably creating a sixth category for marijuana. Or Congress could remove marijuana from the drug schedule and create a separate regulatory scheme. Congress would also have to amend the Controlled Substances Import and Export Act, and the Food and Drug Administration and the Drug Enforcement Administraton would have to set up new controls for the substance passing through the border.

Would regulation increase marijuana use? Perhaps, but judging by how well and truly drugged up we already are, it is tough to imagine that a marginal increase in marijuana use is going to make a meaningful difference. Compared with the tens of thousands of alcohol-related deaths each year in this country, the potential harm of marijuana seems like a trivial concern.

The official figure for annual marijuana-overdose deaths in the US is zero. Marijuana use might lead to tragic levels of snack-food consumption and escalating demand for Scooby-Doo reruns, but compared with the damage we tolerate from alcohol and prescription drugs, this might be a price worth paying. And old concerns about marijuana's role as a "gateway drug" seem increasingly quaint. Most new heroin addicts start out on the prescription drug Oxycotin using a legal prescription from their doctor.

It will not be easy to find the right mix of regulation and availability for narcotics, but we have to start exploring new options. Right now it's easier for high-school kids to buy weed than it is for them to purchase beer or sinus medicine. Finding a way to make marijuana available through a controlled channel makes more sense than devoting $13 billion each year to futile prohibition efforts. When it comes to drug abuse, we have bigger fish to fry ... and they're chock full of Prozac.

Health Care in the Ownership Society

The fundamental problem with health care as a market is that most "consumers" in a medical marketplace are ill, some of them seriously so. A patient's vulnerability creates a coercive effect, which ruins the price-setting mechanisms of a market.

This means that the tools that conservatives love the most in other scenarios fail us here.

We can't simply stand pat. Our current system is an escalating disaster. It is vastly more expensive than anything found elsewhere in the world. Its costs fall heavily on businesses ($500 billion a year) and local governments ($400 billion a year). Our system chains families to an employer, since individual coverage is grotesquely expensive.

Employers are groaning under spectacular costs, while retirement is being priced out of reach by medical costs. And this system punishes the activity that our economy needs most: entrepreneurship.

The Affordable Care Act mitigates some of these problems, but only around the edges and at the price of a spectacular expansion in unsustainable central control. The Affordable Care Act takes the existing health-care model and buries it in a blizzard of bureaucracy. It mandates individual coverage without making that coverage affordable enough for middle-income families that do not receive subsidies. It retains our dependence on employment-based insurance.

The country needs a solution that acknowledges the strengths and weaknesses of our current arrangement along with the political realities than constrain our options. How can we build a system that meets conservative desires for an ownership society and liberal ambitions for universal care?

We start by building from what we have. Looking at some of the world's best health-care systems, we can see a pattern emerge. Each of them evolved from previously existing arrangements, rather than being built from the ground up by legislative action.

What we have currently in the U.S. is a system of socialized medicine based on a matrix of private for-profit providers, private for-profit insurers, and Medicare/Medicaid. The central problems with our system are that it is obscenely expensive, almost double the cost of the world's next most expensive system, and that it fails to cover a large number of citizens. For those inside the coverage matrix, through either an employer or a retirement benefit, our system works well. For those who fall outside this matrix, including entrepreneurs, our health-care system remains a dangerous, expensive mess.

How can this existing system of profit-based providers and insurers be extended to cover everyone? Perhaps like this:

Create a federal program for universal *private* insurance coverage. This program would be funded by a payroll tax, and each state would have to decide whether to participate. This combines characteristics of the French (coverage and service by private providers) and German (coverage and benefits controlled by individual states) systems. The program would fully fund the purchase of a private insurance plan with no additional premiums or deductibles. Any insurer who participated would have to insure everyone, without ratings. The menu of policies would be fairly uniform and would include co-pays to avoid overconsumption.

In effect, every citizen of every participating state would be aggregated into a giant pool. Insurers would operate in a manner similar to our utilities. They would compete on quality of service and derive profit from administrative efficiency.

Medicare and Medicaid would be obsolete, because everyone in the states that opted in would have full private coverage. The programs would be wound down over a five-year period, shrinking the federal workforce by about 8,000 and eliminating $600 billion a year in federal costs. States that chose not to participate in the federal universal-coverage program would be left to replace Medicare and Medicaid on their own.

Some states might opt out in favor of true single-payer health care, as California and Vermont are already trying to do. They would find the process far easier under this system than under our current federally controlled approach. Other states would, well, have to think real hard about whether Rick Perry's approach to government is right for their future.

One main challenge of such a system is that the cost, though cheaper than our present approach, would be relatively transparent and individual, leading to some political difficulties. Our current system evolved in part because of the public's resistance to funding health care. We have a system that socializes the cost of health insurance by concealing it. The cost of this proposal would be squarely in the public eye while the savings would show up in a thousand small ways, hard to notice or appreciate but deeply important.

Research suggests that such a program funded by a flat payroll tax with an income cap of about $250,000 a year would require a tax rate ranging somewhere between 11%–13%. That's consistent with a study done for the state of Minnesota and with the proven cost of the French system. Much of that payroll tax could be paid by employers without significantly burdening individual contractors or entrepreneurs. Their challenge is not so much FICA as the nearly bottomless cost of insurance and the difficulty of obtaining individual coverage.

For an analysis, use the highest cost estimates and assume a system in which the individual payroll-tax burden is 4% and the employer portion is 9%. Then consider the fact that this tax would replace the 3% we already pay in FICA for health care (split between employer and employee). There would also have to be some provision for individuals' capital gains, which would perhaps be taxed at a slightly lower rate.

Cost calculations are too complex to describe in all their detail here, but broad cost estimates would look like this:

Take a family of four earning the 2013 median income of $75,000. They have a better-than-average insurance plan provided by an employer, which costs them $3,600 in annual premiums with a $1,000 deductible. In reasonably healthy years they spend roughly $4,200 on premiums and co-pays. They pay $1,087 in Medicare taxes. Their total annual out-of-pocket for insurance, care, and related FICA taxes is about $5,300.

The employer's cost for a plan this generous is roughly $18,000. The employer pays an additional $1,087 in Medicare taxes for this employee. Under the present system, this family's health care in a healthy year costs the employer about $19,000 (subsidized by a tax deduction) and costs the family directly about $5,300.

This, by the way, illustrates the central political problem with our current health-insurance system. The overwhelming bulk of its cost is invisible to voters. Any health-care reform makes the real cost of U.S. health care (the highest in the world by nearly double) suddenly very obvious.

Under universal private insurance, the family would no longer pay premiums or deductibles. Their 1.45% FICA tax ($1,087) would be replaced with a 4% tax, costing $3,000. They would still have a private insurer of their choice with some responsibility for co-pays. Their average "healthy year" costs would be about $3,600 instead of the $5,300 they pay today. The employer's costs would go from $19,000 to $6,750, and the company would no longer have to shop for health insurers.

The main political challenge with this plan comes from its impact on higher-earners. Families in very good health earning more than about $150,000 (the top 15% of households) who have good insurance from an employer will find that this plan costs them more out of pocket per year than our current system. They will see other benefits from the change, but they may not recognize them.

First, they will never again worry about losing health care if members of the family become unemployed, start a business, or retire. The primary policyholder won't need to carry enough life insurance to cover health-insurance premiums for their survivors. Parents will no longer fear the prospect that a child's illness will destroy their chance for retirement or their ability to pay for college. They will not have to consider the burden of health-insurance premiums when deciding whether they can afford to retire early.

Wealthier taxpayers hit by the new tax would have vastly greater opportunities to semi-retire, work as contractors, or launch a new business, since those choices would not bring the burdensome fixed cost of individual health insurance. And they will live in a country that provides good-quality medical care to all of its citizens without going further into debt.

If the resistance to the new tax burden were strong enough, a state could simply opt-out of the plan and finance medical coverage in another way. There would be a political outlet valve and the possibility that someone could develop a better approach.

The problem of state shopping could be curbed fairly easily by requiring new residents of opt-in states to pay a premium, in addition to the tax, influenced by how many adult years they had been living in an opt-out state. If my income in an opt-out state dropped to zero, I might be attracted to an opt-in state to obtain health care. But if I moved, I would have to pay a health-insurance premium, perhaps $400 a month, for a fraction of the years that I had been living as an adult in an opt-out state under this system. I would also be responsible for a deductible. Still attractive, perhaps, but not exactly a free ride.

This plan could appeal to conservatives by radically shrinking the federal bureaucracy, strengthening small businesses, fostering entrepreneurship, and retaining access to private, for-profit insurers and providers. It would also restore the authority of individual states to build innovative care structures appropriate to their needs.

Liberals would finally get universal, tax-financed health care. Never again would anyone go bankrupt because of an illness in the family. The poor would have access to exactly the same basic care as everyone else.

There would still be hundreds of details to work out, but on the whole this would be far simpler than the Affordable Care Act while covering everyone with private insurance.

Our medical finance system provides quality care to the successfully employed, the elderly, and the wealthy. Everyone else is left to struggle with one stopgap or another. This is a poor practice that has made our system wildly expensive while delivering unimpressive outcomes and dampening business innovation. Most of all, it is morally intolerable.

An ownership society favors policies that expand the range of responsible choices available to everyone and seeks to make us all individually accountable for those choices. The question is not more or less government, but more or less *choice*.

Wherever possible, we steer away from heavily bureaucratic or centralized solutions because we've figured out that a dense, central bureaucracy is too slow to cope with a highly dynamic economy. That said, there is no reason to shy away from a government program if that program makes more personal economic decisions available to individuals.

Our current system for funding health care narrows the choices available to citizens to cope with medical issues. Leaving aside what our current system does to the working poor, it chains workers to an outdated system of employment while punishing those who launch small businesses. There is nothing in the pre-"Obamacare" status quo for Republicans to like, and the Affordable Care Act does not solve the core problems of our system.

Conservatives must abandon their dead-ender commitment to obstructing any and every possible solution to our medical finance problems. It's time to face facts and try to build real-world solutions that can lead to better health outcomes, limit government scope, lower costs, and preserve the greatest possible range of individual autonomy.

Health care is a tough case, but no harder than trying to find a replacement for the welfare state. What if it were possible to close down most of the bureaucracy we devote to welfare and entitlements for the poor while eliminating poverty once and for all?

How to End the Welfare State

How would Republicans react to a proposal that would eliminate the food-stamp program, shut down welfare, slash the state and federal workforce, replace Social Security, and end the minimum wage? How would Democrats respond if that same program extended the social safety net across the entire population, eliminating poverty and fueling opportunity for the less fortunate?

The answer: Both sides would ignore it.

Those seemingly contradictory goals could actually be accomplished with an idea conceived by libertarian economists. Neither major party, nor the Libertarian Party for that matter, has any interest in the idea, but as the "big government" concept falls to pieces under the weight of modern complexity, this approach to social welfare may rescue representative democracy from itself.

Establishing a universal "basic income" would eliminate the administration, politics, and preference that travel in the wake of the welfare state while snuffing out poverty once and for all. Libertarian economist Friederick Hayek described the concept in *Law, Legislation, and Liberty, Vol 3*:

"The assurance of a certain minimum income for everyone, or a sort of floor below which nobody need fall even when he is unable to provide for himself, appears not only to be wholly legitimate protection against a risk common to all, but a necessary part of the Great Society in which the individual no longer has specific claims on the members of the particular small group into which he was born."

Milton Friedman worked with the Nixon administration in 1969 to propose something along these lines, calling it the Family Assistance Plan. The effort failed in Congress, due in large part to Democratic resistance, and has not been revisited in a serious manner.

Friedman's failed effort to craft a basic income did lead to policy changes. In 1975, Congress created something similar based on Friedman's idea for a "negative income tax." The Earned Income Tax Credit delivers an annual payment to working families earning less than the minimum income threshold. The concept is very similar to a basic income, but the credit can only be received by people with a job and very little of this money is available to households without children.

Republicans like Marco Rubio and Paul Ryan have proposed expansions of the EITC as a way of delivering more assistance to low earners. They have stopped short of proposing a universal basic income, though they are inching closer.

Scholars have kept the idea of a minimum income alive. Charles Murray of the American Enterprise Institute has formulated what may be the simplest approach. Murray's plan involves paying every adult, regardless of need, a minimum monthly income sufficient to stave off poverty, probably about $10,000 a year. There are other ways to approach a minimum income that might be much cheaper and probably more politically palatable.

Getting to a politically acceptable proposal starts with understanding the philosophy behind the idea. The goal is to replace the welfare state with a kind of national profit-sharing plan. If we are going to enjoy the massive wealth-creation potential of a highly dynamic capitalist economy, then we can look forward to a world that is vastly richer overall, but far more unequal. That transition will bring a steady erosion of the availability and value of low-skilled jobs and much less job security for everyone. In order to benefit from this transition, people need more education and the ability to launch their careers later in life.

In exchange for embracing the growth potential of a more dynamic economy, ordinary people should be compensated with a more robust safety net and a meaningful stake in the system.

There are many potential ways to structure a basic-income plan. Here's one model that might work: Set the individual basic income at perhaps $15,000, a figure well above the official poverty line. Payments would be triggered not by filing an application or being determined to be "needy," but by monthly income. Anyone whose W2 earnings fell below the threshold for the basic income would receive a payment the following month.

Payments would only be made to adult citizens. There would be no additional money for children. There would be no adjustments for household size or marital status. Earn less than the threshold, get a check.

Eligibility would be phased in and out on a sliding scale, ending at an income of about $30,000 a year. No one would live on less than an annualized amount of 15,000, but those who take home earnings between $1 and $30,000 would receive a subsidy that gradually decreased as their earnings rose. Incentives for work would therefore remain in place.

Those payments would change over time, but instead of tying benefits to inflation as we do with welfare payments, benefits would be tied to GDP or perhaps tax receipts. Payments would move up or down based on a three-year average of national wealth production.

If, as some analysts might fear, a basic income discouraged productive activity to an extent that it impacted the economy, the monthly profit-sharing payments would decline. If the country prospered, the less fortunate would prosper along with it.

How many people would be eligible for this subsidy? More than you might imagine.

Well over half of working Americans earn less than $30,000 a year. Eighty-five percent of U.S. workers earn less than $70,000. Roughly 120 million American adults would qualify for either a full basic income or some subsidy. So what would it cost us to provide a basic income?

The cost would run about $1.8 trillion. However, when compared with some of the savings, it begins to look extremely attractive.

A basic income would completely replace welfare and Social Security spending, freeing up hundreds of billions of dollars and radically shrinking the federal government. Keep in mind that the average Social Security retirement benefit is almost exactly the same amount as the basic-income proposal discussed here.

The current annual budget for Social Security is more than $800 billion. More than $12 billion of that money is spent on administration alone. Another $400 billion is spent on a galaxy of poverty-assistance programs like food stamps and welfare. Replacing our existing social safety net with a universal income could displace more than $1.2 trillion in existing spending.

The remaining $600 billion of the cost could be split in a way that was shared across the economy. Half of the money could come from a modest income-tax increase while the rest could come from sales taxes.

A 15% tax increase (not a 15-*point* increase, but rates 15% higher than our current structure) would generate roughly $300 billion. That means an earner in the top 5% who currently pays on average almost 21% of their income in federal income tax would instead pay roughly 24%. A VAT or sales tax of 6% would generate the other $300 billion. Social Security payroll taxes would be eliminated.

Think about that for a minute. Basically, by adding a 6% national sales tax and paying roughly three percentage points more per year in income tax we could end the welfare state as we know it, end poverty, slash the size of the state and federal bureaucracy, and shrink government to a pre–World War II scale. It is solid value for the money.

The idea is not unprecedented. Alaska has had a form of minimum income for more than 30 years. Revenue from state-owned natural resources is pooled in a sovereign wealth fund. A portion of the fund is paid out to every resident in an annual payment.

Brazil has been working with a basic-income program for more than a decade. The country's program is means-tested and includes significant behavioral qualifications. The money goes to families who have their children vaccinated and keep them in school. That program has been wildly successful by nearly any measure. Britain is introducing a variation on the basic-income concept called a "universal tax credit," designed to consolidate welfare programs and cut costs.

Despite the potential advantages, neither side of the political spectrum is offering much, if any, support for this concept. The pursuit of such an ambitious plan, for all its promise, raises valid questions, some of which are nearly impossible to answer with certainty.

How would our lives, economy, and culture change if no one ever faced the possibility of being penniless? By opening up basic support to everyone, would we see massive new influx of entrepreneurship and risk-taking, or a great new age of sitting on the couch consuming entertainment?

Traditional conservatives are queasy about a basic income because it replaces one massive social engineering scheme with what they perceive as brand new massive social engineering scheme. Liberals resist removing government from its nanny role. They fear the impact of an ownership-oriented social safety net, worrying that the lives of the poor would get worse without the benevolent guidance of government bureaucrats.

Circumstances may soon force a closer look at this solution. A minimum income is capitalism's answer to the social safety net. Socialism tries to solve the problems of inequality and poverty by having the state seize control over capital. In a socialist system, the state owns the major means of production, workers are usually forced to join a union, and everyone is guaranteed employment.

A basic income takes the opposite approach in every respect. Capital remains entirely in private hands. Workers make their own employment decisions. Unlike socialism, a basic income leaves most of the economy untouched.

Under a basic income, people do what they want with their capital and with their lives. The safety net is paid for with income and consumption taxes, not with state ownership of capital. This approach delivers more individual freedom, less bureaucracy, and a powerful social safety net. The dynamism of a free economy remains intact while more choices are made available to everyone. There is plenty here to like for people all over the political spectrum.

When the subject of a basic income comes up, people immediately worry about idleness, but the impact of an income floor on ambitious people with few family resources could be enormous. Sure, it would help the poor, but the poor already have access to a lot of help. The biggest impact might be felt by young people from middle-income families struggling to get to the first rung of the economic ladder.

One of the most powerful drivers of income inequality in America is unequal access to education. This has less to do with problems with K–12 education than with the intense pressure to find a paying job too early.

Children from more affluent families have one vital gift that helps them find their way to meaningful work—time. Very few young people, even if they can obtain a college degree, have truly marketable skills. In a knowledge-driven economy, time is the critical element that lets young people cross the chasm to a productive career. One of the great benefits of affluence is the opportunity to do low-paid or unpaid work for extended periods without falling into poverty.

Young people from middle- and lower-income households do not have time. They must earn money to live long before they can acquire the skills to earn money well. We lose their potential contribution. Forcing young people too soon into low-wage, low-value work is maddeningly counterproductive and ultimately expensive.

Conservatives who worry about people not working under a basic-income proposal often spend much of their day worrying about the supposed decline in "family values." Ironically, a basic income is probably the best friend of family values.

If you want an accurate picture of what someone values, watch where they spend their money. Our leaders almost universally praise parents who stay home to care for children. Meanwhile we punish these parents in every conceivable way. A woman

129

who can earn a six-figure salary as an attorney will earn nothing for devoting her talents and energy to being a mother. Forget all the talk; that's the truest picture of what we value as a culture. A basic income would change that.

A basic income would at least provide some subsidy available for a father or mother who decided not to work, or to work in a very limited way, while raising children. They wouldn't get additional money for having children (depending on the plan), but they would not go without an income.

Would fewer people work? Would a lot of people shirk? Who cares?

Is it worthwhile to waste hundreds of billions of dollars and support a vast, powerful, and largely unnecessary bureaucracy to assure ourselves that no one out there is getting a few extra dollars? Whoever is content to stay home and smoke weed all day while living on $15,000 a year is probably not crucial to our economic future. Their consumption is more valuable than their labor. Stop worrying about them.

Why shouldn't a minimum income have a work requirement, similar to EITC-based proposals from Senator Rubio and Representative Ryan? Because that approach is merely flipping the subsidy, granting taxpayer money to companies that benefit from underpaying workers. Whereas a minimum income places choices and options in the hands of low-income individuals—many of whom, let's remember, are just people in their 20s finding their first foothold in the economy—an enhanced EITC takes away their options. It places millions of people at the mercy of WalMart and McDonald's while stifling innovation.

The vast majority of jobs paying less than $10 an hour exist only because they are subsidized by taxpayers through our current safety net. Raise the minimum wage and create a basic income, and your fast food will be delivered by the McDonaldtron 3000 and your order will always be right. The high-value jobs and innovation stimulated by a smaller workforce will generate far more economic value than forcing low-income people into meaningless work. Out of a strange, misguided jealousy toward the poor, we are weakening our own collective ability to innovate and compete globally.

Proposals like a basic income open a window to adaptation that could preserve the features we value in our government while stripping away much of its ponderous bulk. The idea deserves serious consideration.

A few notes about "income redistribution"

These proposals for universal health care and a replacement of the welfare state might offend a sizable block of conservatives. Opposition to anything that smacks of "income redistribution" has been a defining trait of the right in recent years. Never mind what a program might accomplish—even radically shrinking the federal government and expand liberty for everyone—whenever we raise taxes we are supporting "socialism" and "government dependence."

Income redistribution is one of the principle functions of civilization. It's what America does and Somalia and Haiti do not do. At the very least, every functioning government collects income from taxes and redistributes it to fund essential infrastructure that benefits everyone. Americans of all income groups and political parties benefit from income redistribution all the livelong day. If income redistribution makes people "dependent" on government, then humankind has been universally "dependent" since we gave up hunting mammoths for food.

Indeed, income redistribution is the reason those highly independent red-state conservatives who live on farms far from cities and claim they need nothing from the government have access to electricity, roads, hospitals, schools, doctors, telephones, and the Internet. Not to mention that without direct government subsidies, most of what remains of family farming in this country would disappear overnight.

Never mind the more-obvious examples of benefits like roads, police, and courts. Without income redistribution in the form of government agencies, mortgage-market supports, and very generous tax subsidies, there would be practically no middle-class homeownership in this country. The elderly, other than those who are extremely wealthy, would not be able to afford modern medical care in almost any form. Almost none of the medicines you use would have been invented. Without income redistribution, very few of us would be capable of reading this.

If you doubt your own government dependence, consider this example. I'm a white married suburbanite with a great job who lives in a really nice neighborhood. My house is surrounded by a white picket fence—no kidding. I haven't broken into the 1% just yet, but I have ambitions.

I am the face of the Welfare State. And so are you.

I earn tax deductions for the courageous public service of holding a mortgage. I get tax credits for having kids. The government credits me money for contributing to a retirement account. Tax deductions subsidize my medical costs through a convenient flexible-spending card, and tax deductions help me pay my health-insurance premiums.

My work would be impossible without a communications infrastructure built largely with taxpayer money, developed with taxpayer-funded research, and maintained in part by a taxpayer-funded bureaucracy. Without money taken from taxpayers by the government and redistributed to build highways and airports, I could not meet clients.

At different times in my life, taxpayers have helped me pay for day care and student-loan interest. And it doesn't stop there. Taxpayers are going to help me buy a beach house by subsidizing my interest payments, taxes, and maintenance costs.

Just like the coffee I drink, my entitlements aren't cheap. The mortgage-interest deduction by itself costs the taxpayers *more than the entire food-stamp program.* Even at the depth of the Great Recession, with enrollment at a record high, food stamps cost $78 billion a year, compared with $100 billion for the mortgage interest credit. That's right, we spend more money helping middle- and upper-income Americans buy homes (and vacation homes) than we spend providing food to poor people. Federal "tax expenditures," those myriad little giveaways that reduce personal and corporate tax payments, cost more than $1 trillion dollars a year—twice as much as Medicare does.

Furthermore, a large chunk of the food-stamp budget goes to support working households. Forty percent of the "takers" on the food-stamp programs are families working hard to make ends meet. And how high are these "moochers" living? In Texas, for example, the average monthly benefit is $125 a month. Have fun feeding your family on that. Most food-stamp recipients are white, and a large minority is "working poor."

Our challenge is not to wean people off of "government dependence." We are all utterly dependent on a successful government for our basic quality of life. Government welfare programs should be focused on making all Americans *more independent,* with greater options to use our talents and efforts toward our own personal goals. Our purpose should be to build an optimistic system in which all forms of government activity, from food stamps to small-business loans, function more like a trampoline and less like a spider web. Along the way we should be looking for ways to make government actions more efficient, smarter, and more sustainable by cutting unnecessary cost and bureaucracy.

Our policies on income redistribution will decide the range and scope of our individual choices. Will those choices be constantly more constrained by a large, distant government bureaucracy, or will we have the intelligence to embrace approaches to income redistribution that lead to ever-expanding personal freedom?

Using Markets to Protect the Environment

Operating an industrial boiler requires skill and experience, not to mention the significant capital outlay required to obtain one. It also requires something else: adherence to a lengthy set of operating rules laid out and frequently updated by the U.S. Environmental Protection Agency.

But hardly anyone with the requisite skills to manage an industrial boiler is also gifted with the specialized knowledge required to fully understand the EPA's nearly 100 pages of detailed operating rules, or to properly interpret their intentions and implications. To own and operate an industrial boiler, you also need a good attorney.

Virtually no corner of industrial operations in the United States is free to operate without consulting a dense thicket of operating rules issued by regulators at the federal, state, and even local level. Those rules are designed to protect workers from injury, reduce pollution, prevent fraud, and accomplish any number of other laudable goals.

It is very difficult for a highly educated and trained scientist with a keen understanding of the impact of sulfur dioxide on the atmosphere to draft detailed operating instructions for a power plant without wreaking havoc on that plant's operations. The challenge comes less from an understanding of how a smokestack works than from the speed of technological advancement.

A regulatory code, like a package of computer code, is stupid—it does not think or adapt or evolve on its own. The process of developing a code of regulations for something as complex as an industrial boiler is extremely time-consuming. In an economy as dynamic as ours, rules are often dated by the time they take effect.

As the complexity of our economy and our lives accelerates, the cost of regulation is skyrocketing. Fortunately, there is an alternative. We have already used it successfully in a few limited settings, and it is perfectly suited to tackle our most challenging, complex, and dangerous pollution challenge—climate change.

Markets are much smarter than regulatory codes because they are, essentially, alive. If the rules of a market can be set to include the price of pollution, then markets could be made to do much of the work that otherwise falls to regulators.

Trading of pollution credits, for example, has been the key to a massive reduction in acid rain caused by sulfur and nitrogen oxides released from coal-burning power plants. The program worked like this: Instead of issuing a new set of detailed regulations forcing power plants to adopt this or that technique for reducing emissions, the EPA set a new cap on sulfur-dioxide emissions. Companies that lowered their emissions below the cap could sell their additional polluting capacity to other companies that had failed to meet the targets. This created a market in pollution reduction with a very impressive side benefit—new capital investment in innovation aimed at pollution reduction.

Regulators were freed from the tedious and increasingly futile challenge of writing rules that companies were constantly working to evade. Companies were released to find the best possible solution to their emissions problem and a new business model emerged around emissions reduction.

Since the plan was placed into effect, sulfur-dioxide emissions from the plants covered by the program have decreased by more than half. Pollution trading has clearly had a significant, sustained positive impact.

Instead of saddling power plants with the burden of additional operating rules that could not possibly have adapted fast enough to keep pace with innovation, plant owners were able to capitalize on the most suitable remediation for their needs. And nonprofit organizations have participated in these markets by purchasing pollution credits, raising the price of the credits and taking additional sulfur pollution out of the system. This gives environmental groups an additional avenue to directly impact on levels of pollution.

How much has cap and trade added to the cost of energy in the U.S.? Slashing sulfur pollution by more than half has cost a few cents per kilowatt hour. The cost has been virtually invisible to consumers, a fraction of the cost of an ongoing dance between regulators and polluters. And it has been radically effective.

Challenges still exist in implementing such a scheme. A cap-and-trade approach does not immediately ban pollution. Pricing can be complex. It is possible to set the cap too high, which allows polluters to "bank" credits, slowing pollution reduction over time. Set the cap too low, and the costs could become ruinous. Market-based regulation cannot entirely replace traditional regulation, but it offers an opportunity to meet public needs in an increasingly complex economy not just regarding pollution, but also in banking, employment safety, and other efforts. Overall, though, perhaps the most promising opportunity is in climate change.

What a carbon market might look like

Building on the success of market-based approaches to pollution control, policy makers on the right pressed for years for America to adopt a similar approach to control carbon emissions. Their efforts were close to success in 2008, when both U.S. presidential candidates backed their plans. But

136

carbon trading as national-scale solution has disappeared in the past few years as the Republican grassroots has lined up almost entirely behind a denialist agenda on climate change. Yet carbon trading remains the most promising proposal for reducing carbon emissions. We just need to find the will to implement it.

Climate change is a particularly difficult pollution problem. Our economy is tuned to run on fossil fuels. Our regulatory environment, tax incentives, and federal, state, and local transportation planning and infrastructure are all programmed to facilitate the delivery and use of carbon-based fuels.

No alternative technology yet exists that could fully replace our reliance on carbon-emitting fuels today. Once that technology emerges, it will likely require new infrastructure for exploitation and delivery, requiring expensive new capital development. Whatever we do to develop alternative sources, we will face a near-term future in which almost every human activity is affected by dependence on oil, natural gas, or coal.

We must work to mitigate the growing impact of the carbon pollution already in our atmosphere while we explore alternative energy sources. As in the problem of sulfur-dioxide pollution and acid rain, markets could deliver a more efficient outcome for carbon reduction than could heavy-handed bureaucratic intervention.

Left alone, markets will not price in the future costs of climate change. Free markets will not assign any value to elements external to a transaction between a self-interested buyer and seller. Dead polar bears and a flooded Miami will not influence the value of energy transactions on global markets without some regulatory effort.

But by using the Pigovian pricing tools refined in the fight to control acid rain, the U.S. could create a market price for carbon reduction. The process would start with a carbon cap.

The federal government would then assign a tax on carbon emissions, applied to the fuel producers at the point of production or import, for production above that ceiling. To make the program work, import tariffs would have to be levied on goods from countries that do not apply a similar scheme.

Revenues generated from the tax should be directed toward alternative-energy research and efforts to mitigate the damage from climate change. With a market for carbon reduction, new tactics and technologies would emerge fairly quickly to reduce carbon emissions and capture carbon already in the atmosphere. This process has been stunted to date by lack of capital available for investment in these technologies. The presence of a potential profit would remove that obstacle.

The alternative course is new regulation of power plants, new regulations on energy production, government-funded capital investments on technologies chosen by bureaucrats rather than markets, and an all-around increase in bureaucratic interference in energy markets. Not every problem can be solved with a market, but where market options are available we should embrace them Climate change is a perfect opportunity to let innovation reduce the cost of regulation.

Building a Market for Gun Safety

Carbon pollution is a technically complex problem with a potentially simple, market-based political solution. America's problem with gun deaths has a technically simple problem that sits behind a nightmarishly thorny political tangle. Nevertheless, just like climate change, markets may provide the best solution to the challenge of effective gun control.

In many parts of America it is tougher to get a driver's license than it is to buy an assault rifle. No one complains about the need to license drivers or the requirement that each automobile owner maintain insurance to cover the damage he or she might cause with the vehicle. Cars have considerable potential to cause death or injury. To let people use them at full discretion without training or a guarantee of personal liability would be patently absurd.

Meanwhile we suffer levels of gun violence that would be extreme in a country at war. A massive majority of the public wants stricter laws in place to protect us from the pointless death and injury we endure. Those who value gun ownership are building up a costly backlash by opposing pretty much any reasonable effort to contain the slaughter in the interest of virtually unregulated gun ownership.

As gun deaths continue to rise and auto safety steadily improves, gun fatalities are on a pace to take more American lives in 2015 than car accidents. What if we learned from our experience with automotive safety and regulated guns like cars? What if ownership was open to every adult who could prove basic capabilities and obtain personal-liability insurance? Holding gun owners financially accountable through the same structures we use for other potentially dangerous products like automobiles could drastically reduce deaths while preserving the basic right to own a weapon.

In an ownership culture, government does less to dictate individual choices and more to ensure accountability, transparency, and responsibility. Those values are sorely lacking in current gun laws and almost completely absent from proposals under consideration.

Our current gun laws create a thicket of largely artificial, ineffectual, and often deliberately unenforceable rules riddled with loopholes. They are practically engineered to create the impression that only criminals can obtain a weapon. Strict compliance with the laws is impossible due to their complexity and contradictions.

Colorado's weak new gun laws are intended to block the sale of "high capacity" magazine clips. In the process they ban any form of magazine that can be "readily converted" to accommodate higher capacities. That provision effectively bans all gun magazines, making the entire provision unenforceable in practical terms.

The assault-weapons ban, which Congress allowed to expire during the Bush administration, was even worse. It was written to ban weapons that had two or more characteristics from a given list. Its terminology was too general to be consistently applied, yet the punishments for violating these impossibly confusing rules were draconian. Our legal codes are packed with attempts to regulate guns, meanwhile our streets are flooded with legal and illegal weapons. Our approach to this problem is a lethal failure.

Laws also severely limit the ability of police to track weapons and identify and prosecute illegal dealers. As a consequence, we have not only allowed our country to be overrun with firepower, we have become a primary arms market for criminals in neighboring countries.

New proposals would add more symbolic regulation on top of existing symbolic regulation. For example, an assault-weapons ban sounds useful until you look at how vague the restrictions are. It is easy to circumvent them and also easy to accidentally violate them. Background checks are a modest help at the moment of purchase, but they don't follow that gun through its lifespan. Our thinking about weapons regulation fails to address the need for choice bounded by accountability, transparency, and responsibility.

We need a new approach, but the effort to craft better laws is complicated by relative indifference to gun rights on one side and tin-hat paranoia on the other. Borrowing on what we've learned from a century of dealing with automobile safety, here's an idea that might work.

First, loosen most of the explicit federal curbs related to functionality, shape, and other characteristics of guns. They sound like great ideas, but they do not work. While failing to keep dangerous weapons out of the wrong hands, they needlessly entangle responsible gun owners. And with appropriate accountability in place, those restrictions become largely meaningless.

In the interest of accountability and transparency, establish a formal, national gun registry with owners' names and weapons' serial numbers. That registry should have roughly the same privacy protections we give to medical records and would be accessible by law enforcement and insurers. Building and maintaining the registry would be expensive. It could be funded by a sales tax on ammunition.

Owning an unregistered weapon would be a federal crime, punishable by imprisonment. Owners would be personally accountable for weapons registered to them, and would bear civil liability for crimes or injuries resulting from the use of weapons registered to them. They would be responsible to notify authorities within a fixed time, perhaps seven days, of any theft or loss in order to avoid liability for crimes or injuries caused by a lost or stolen weapon.

Gun owners would be responsible financially for their choices, too. No weapon could be registered or remain registered without proof of liability insurance provided annually. Lapsed insurance would be a crime which could be remedied by surrendering the uninsured weapons, paying a bond (self-insurance), or facing penalties for unlicensed possession. It would also be a federal crime to sell a weapon to a buyer who could not demonstrate that they were insured for that weapon.

Gun ownership would cease to be a casual choice like buying a fishing pole, but it would still be available to those who handle the right responsibly. Ted Nugent would have to divert a hefty percentage of the annual royalties from *Cat Scratch Fever* toward insuring his arsenal, but as long as he could afford the duties of responsible ownership, The Nuge could keep whatever guns he wants.

The registration and insurance requirements would make it very difficult for irresponsible or unstable owners to maintain a hoard of weapons. Given the harm that can flow from the careless use of firearms, you can be sure that gun insurance would require proof of safety measures. Markets would make gunlocks, biometric ID systems, and other security and safety measures suddenly almost unavoidable for any gun owner. How many muttering lunatics will master the requirements necessary to prove competent gun ownership to an insurance company that would be liable for their actions?

Anyone who owned a large arsenal or began acquiring numerous weapons in a short time would see their premiums escalate, and potentially have their insurer withdraw coverage. With every weapon accounted for, anyone who had coverage revoked could draw police attention quickly. A gun owner who was falling apart mentally or failing to take reasonable safety precautions would probably start getting attention from the authorities long before they, or someone with access to their weapons, shot up a movie theater.

State and local governments might enact additional requirements, within the bounds of a general right to gun ownership, or they might not. It would probably be much harder to carry a weapon in Manhattan than in Wyoming, as is entirely appropriate. That's federalism.

The choice to own almost any type of gun would remain, but it would be bounded by responsibilities. That is what liberty looks like to a traditional conservative. Those wise enough to exercise their freedom responsibly would enjoy nearly unlimited rights of gun ownership. Those who behave irresponsibly would see their options constrained, in many cases before they caused irreparable harm to someone else.

As for my untrammeled right to own any weapon I want with no accountability or regulation, that does not exist and has never existed. As for my right to hold weapons as a method of "defending" myself from my elected government, that does not exist and has never existed. It is not in the Constitution or the Bill of Rights and never has been found under any Constitutional interpretation we have ever used. Pack the Supreme Court with nine Scalias, and you still won't have those rights. Such claims run counter to the any conservative notion of liberty. Where we are free, we are accountable. Freedom, as we like to say, is not free. Freedom is bounded by our duties to one another.

In more-practical terms, if someone actually believes that they're going to defend themselves from President Obama with their cache of AR-15s and a cellar full of canned goods, there's little to discuss. No weapon ever developed can shoot down the black helicopters that hover silently over their dreams. Private military arsenals do not guarantee our freedom. The wise use of our political power and the protection of our basic institutions preserve liberty for ourselves and our children.

It is true that no proposal this sweeping could make it through our current Congress. In fairness though, almost nothing can. Congress can't even pass a budget. When our partisan political logjam clears, and it will, this framework might be the best hope for preserving relatively broad personal gun ownership for the long term.

Under this set of rules, America would remain the most heavily armed nation in the developed world by a vast margin, but we could have far less mayhem. Choice, accountability, transparency, and responsibility: these values of the ownership society could drastically reduce the cost and carnage of unregulated weaponry while preserving America's unique relationship to personal firearms.

Social Conservatives, Candy Cigarettes, and the Ownership Society

Growing up, there was a U-Totem just a block from my cousin's trailer park. We used to walk there to buy candy cigarettes and a brand of gum that came in a fake Skoal can.

I developed a pack-a-day candy-cigarette habit on my summer visits.

Apparently those chalky sugar cigarettes I loved as a kid were never outlawed. I found them recently in a specialty candy store in Nashville. My kids couldn't grasp the appeal. When I showed them the candy they looked at me like I was offering them a box of spiders and warily refused the treat.

Social conservatives could learn a lot from public health-and-safety campaigns of the last generation. Those efforts had relatively modest legislative support but transformed our culture at its core in a very short time. Instead of leading with prohibition, they chipped away at the culture with a steady onslaught of reason, science, and careful political pressure. Anti-tobacco activists successfully slashed the incidence of a practice that was not only a cultural icon, but a physical addiction.

When stripped of hysteria and explicitly religious framing, the core concerns of social conservatives are perhaps more popular than they have ever been. Yet social conservatives are a serious electoral drag. Values voters might be able to promote their agenda more successfully if they could distance themselves from authoritarian policies that frighten voters.

Social conservatism, at its best, represents an optimism born of the understanding that law can never be separated from morality and that right always prevails over time. To borrow Dr. King's phrase, the arc of the moral universe is long, but it bends toward justice. Confidence in this belief, when embraced, gives rise to an open-minded fearlessness that forms a powerful draw. There is much in our modern era to fuel this kind of optimism.

Unfortunately, social conservatives are not always at their best. A prominent strain of the movement exists in permanent tension with representative government. Some believe that mankind is so terminally corrupt that our choices ought to be severely constrained. Government, their reasoning goes, should actively promote the only true and legitimate source of moral authority. That legitimate source, by happy coincidence, springs from careful observance of the social conservatives' religious heritage.

To that way of thinking, tolerating a certain degree of public impiety might be necessary in the interests of liberty, but each such compromise brings with it a dire threat of moral degradation, dangerous to the very survival of the state. They believe that strong, healthy, vibrant states are pious states. Piety by individual choice might be nice, but piety is too important to be left to chance. Old-school social conservatives generally believe that piety by legislation and state coercion is usually necessary. Impiety is not to be tolerated, or divine wrath awaits.

By that logic, social conservatism becomes an expression of cultural or racial fears. It leads directly to authoritarian oppression. Our Founders understood this keenly, having lived under its consequences. That is why they worked so hard to keep religion at a safe distance from political authority. Unfortunately, this authoritarian brand of "social conservatism" thrives when intense social change leaves people feeling overwhelmed and threatened. This is one of those times.

No one should be surprised at the wave of religious fundamentalism we are experiencing in the U.S. Until the Future Shock generation passes the peak of its political sway, fundamentalism will influence politics, though its power is already waning.

An ownership society places culture in a very different light than traditional social conservatives do. With an emphasis on individual choices, values come to be weighed on the basis of their results rather than their divine credentials. Personal moral choices that yield a better, happier, healthier lifestyle are sought after and respected regardless of their religious pedigree.

A social conservative from the '70s, plopped down into our age, might be thrilled by what they found as most of the greatest fears of their era have faded. Divorce rates have not only leveled off, but declined. Children are treated with near-reverence, buckled up, cherished, and sheltered from negative influences. New York's Times Square, once a seedy symbol of cultural decay, has become a '70s conservative's wildest fantasy made real.

The rise of substance abuse, crime, and smoking has not just halted but reversed. Public disapproval of adultery has strengthened. Abortion is in steady, long-term decline. Teen sexual activity and pregnancy are dropping.

Our visitor from the '70s would be treated to one particularly mind-boggling phenomenon. Homosexuals are pressing for the right to settle down in stable families and raise children. The Village People now have entirely different plans for the YMCA—signing their kids up for soccer and gymnastics.

By most reasonable measures, social conservatism has experienced a generation of triumph. So why are today's family-values advocates such a gloomy bunch?

While family values have triumphed and spread, organized religion is in steep decline, breeding intense insecurity among many of the hard-core faithful. Social conservatism can be confident when its goals are rooted in the real world of rational, measurable outcomes, but there is a tendency among the rigidly religious to view the wider world with fear rather than confidence. And when social conservatism becomes dominated by insecurity, dark authoritarian impulses emerge.

Social conservatism, at its worst, can be a political gateway drug, paving the way toward fascism. When "values voters" are motivated primarily by fear, their political movements descend into identity politics. If the goal of social conservatives is to enforce sectarian religious values across the entire culture, the movement is doomed.

However, shrill, desperate, intolerant politics is not an inevitable destiny for social conservatives. A potential mission exists for social conservatives willing to pursue "family values" without the sectarian agenda. Lower-income Americans are seeing their lifestyle and opportunities decline relative to the more affluent. Lower earners are seeing every pillar of their social networks crumble under the pressure of falling wages for unskilled labor, rising education costs, and the growing challenge of obtaining quality health care. In those communities, family life and traditional values are diminishing along with their economic prospects.

Among those who are struggling to survive, many of the positive cultural trends that have improved the quality of life for everyone else are nowhere in evidence. Social conservatives have a potential role to play in spreading values that not only promote basic family welfare, but also improve the chances of material success.

There is an insight preserved by social conservatives that could be valuable to struggling communities: Moral values play a crucial role in economic success. In other words, problems facing lower-income Americans cannot be solved with government programs alone. By the same token, they cannot be solved with a reflective urge to prohibit, repress, and scourge.

As David Frum once explained, "If social conservatives can shift away from the urge to ban and condemn, and instead think more about how to support and encourage, they can be a rich source of inspiration for the larger conservative world and the Republican party in the years ahead."

A broad swath of Americans of all ethnicities and religions are open to the core values of social conservatism: family, faith, work and patriotism. The measurable power of delayed gratification and concern for others is a concept social conservatives could spread. An overwhelming majority of Americans are spiritual and values-oriented, prepared to sacrifice their own personal desires to support their families. At the same time, they are generally hostile toward arrogant religious scolds who want to use the political process to impose their sectarian beliefs on others.

Can social conservatives overcome their urge to write religious dogma into legislation and instead use their influence to shore up traditional social and economic values in struggling communities? Can the lessons of the past generation's science- and reason-focused health campaigns form a blueprint for a new era of conservative priorities? Their success proves that a values campaign can succeed if it is based on something more universal than personal religious convictions.

With the right approach and a healthy dose of humility, social conservatives could have a very bright political future. You don't need to pry the candy cigarettes from my cold, dead hands to change public attitudes. Persuasion is more powerful than prohibition in changing a culture.

Why Not Libertarianism?

"[Liberty is] that condition of men in which coercion of some by others is reduced as much as is possible in society" — F.A. Hayek, *The Constitution of Liberty*

Beneath the roiling surface of American partisan rivalry is an emerging consensus informed largely by libertarian ideas. The left often borrows from libertarians on social policy while the right is drawn to their emphasis on markets, but neither side is seizing the opportunity to bridge traditional partisan boundaries with libertarian proposals.

What's missing from libertarian politics is a willingness to adapt to real-world conditions. If libertarians on the right and left of our policy spectrum ever learn how to compromise, they could tap into an emerging public consensus, unleashing a revolution in American politics. Unfortunately, much work remains to be done before we see a version of libertarianism that can function on the ground.

The old Chicago-school libertarianism of Hayek and Friedman was dominated by some very serious thinkers. They were willing to wrestle with the real world in order to move abstract ideas into practical, workable policies. Hayek's definition of liberty, quoted at the top of this chapter, speaks volumes. First, it recognizes that threats to liberty do not come exclusively from government. More important, *his definition is relative, not absolute.* He acknowledged that some degree of coercion is inevitable in order to maintain civilized society. Early Chicago-school scholars sought to make freedom real under the constraints of the world as we experience it.

Freedom from government is not liberty, per se. The goals of liberty are achieved when people have the widest possible range of personal choices available to them. Creating that range of choices often requires the intervention of a central authority. That reality is most apparent when examining the history of African Americans.

You won't find a lot of blacks at a Libertarian Party event. Libertarian politics runs counter to every lesson learned by African Americans in the real-world struggle for civil rights. The long, sad decline of the Republican Party as the primary vehicle of black political expression corresponds closely to the rise of libertarian philosophy as a force in Republican politics. It is a story of unintended consequences, a warning to those who admire many of the better qualities of libertarian philosophy.

Republicans began embracing libertarianism about a decade before the term found its modern American meaning. Republican presidential nominee Barry Goldwater promoted individual liberty as a paramount political value in the early '60s. Libertarians formed a separate political party in the early '70s when a small core of antiwar conservatives broke from the Soviet hawks over Vietnam, but the two movements never fully disentangled from each other.

To this day, figures like Ron Paul and Gary Johnson move easily between Libertarian and Republican circles because the boundaries are muddy. The libertarian movement today is still the heir of the Goldwater Republicans. It was Goldwater who launched the Republican shift toward libertarianism, and it was under Goldwater that the libertarians failed Black America.

The proposed Civil Rights Act of 1964 presented the libertarian wing of the conservative movement with a wrenching choice. Libertarians loathed segregation, but breaking Jim Crow would demand a sweeping expansion of federal power. The dilemma was that African Americans' repression rose not only from government, *but from the culture and personal choices of their white neighbors.*

The Civil Rights Acts proposed to do something that libertarian ideology insisted was impossible—expand personal freedom by expanding federal power. Goldwater made a fateful decision to break from the core of the Republican Party and oppose the 1964 Civil Rights Act. His decision alienated the black community and shone a glaring light on a fatal weakness in libertarian theory.

Goldwater was not a racist. He was troubled by the ideological dilemma he faced. The Civil Rights Acts of '64 and '65 regulated how personal opinions could be expressed in almost any economic terms. Freedom of association, as it had been previously interpreted, was deeply curtailed. The rights of state and local governments were severely limited. Civil-rights legislation was even interpreted to define, in some circumstances, how religious opinions could be expressed.

From the vantage point of history, we can see the results. This dramatic expansion of federal power brought a revolutionary expansion of personal liberty. That's a conundrum for libertarians, for whom freedom is almost always defined by the extent to which individuals are unencumbered by the coercive power of government. By that absurdly narrow definition, the Civil Rights Acts were a dramatic reduction in freedom. Libertarians' obsession with government leaves them blind to other, more powerful forces that destroy personal liberty.

By libertarian standards, Southern states in the pre-civil-rights era were a paradise of personal liberty. There was virtually no government to speak of. Personal choices were almost entirely unburdened by intervention from an organized central authority.

Want to dig a coal mine? Go for it. Want to dump industrial waste in the river? What you do with your property is your own business. Want to lynch a black teenager for whistling at a white girl? No one is going to stop you.

In the libertarian paradise of the Old South, no central authority interfered with a man's basic freedoms. In practical terms, the most powerful political figure in Southern politics was the county sheriff. As a result, the strong, the popular, the well-organized, and the wealthy were able to run roughshod over those with less power.

Enforcement and maintenance of white supremacy did not come from the state. Governments in the South were too weak to enforce anything. Jim Crow was conceived, implemented, and held in place by informal, voluntary, popular arrangements, as one would expect in a libertarian community.

A dense, organic network of paramilitary and terrorist groups performed the day-to-day work of maintaining white supremacy. The Ku Klux Klan is by far the best-known of these organizations, but much of the dirty work of maintaining segregation was carried out by local, less formal groups.

Sitting above the paramilitaries were more-dignified, "moderate" local assemblies, like the White Citizens' Councils of the late Jim Crow period. The secrecy of the paramilitaries meant that a man could sit on a respected assembly by day, urging the peaceful resolution of differences, while also coordinating or even participating in violent activities at night.

Remarkably little of the structure of Jim Crow was ever reduced to law. The laws were only necessary to limit the ability of high-minded law enforcement from attempting to restrain "public will." Jim Crow was almost entirely informal, cultural, and driven by extra-legal enforcement. Jim Crow is a real-world example of what happens under the most extreme forms of libertarianism.

Libertarianism protects personal liberty from being impaired *by government*. It creates weak states on the assumption that without government intrusion personal freedom will blossom.

Emmitt Till was murdered for allegedly whistling at a white woman. The murder was committed by private actors. Their actions were illegal, but government officials at every level, from the sheriff to the U.S. president, were too weak to enforce the law and protect the basic human rights of Till and any other African American in the South.

When Dr. Martin Luther King Jr. rallied African Americans to resist Jim Crow, they faced some resistance from local law enforcement, but it wasn't a sheriff who murdered Emmett Till. No civil authority bombed churches or lynched civil-rights workers. When local law enforcement feebly tried to enforce the law, attempting to prosecute those who harassed or even murdered civil-rights workers, they were thwarted by a liberty-loving community bent on preserving their own freedom to discriminate.

Jim Crow was imposed socially, through local networks rather than officially, through a hierarchy. It began with mobs and was merely decorated, not imposed, by law. And mobs delivered the deadly energy for its defense in the '60s. The "culture war" that emerged from the effort to defeat Jim Crow still refuses to die out.

The libertarianism Goldwater embraced in '64 had its eyes fixed firmly on communism. In the fight against the tyranny of a totalitarian ideology, the right failed to recognize that tyranny can flourish under a weak state. Libertarian conservatives watched Medgar Evers's funeral without recognizing small-government oppression at work.

The high-minded pursuit of personal freedom *from* government made Goldwater an accidental hero for segregationists. In the most noxious irony of the 1964 election, Goldwater as the standard-bearer of personal liberty earned the endorsement of segregationist Democrat Strom Thurmond and became the first Republican to win the Deep South since Reconstruction.

Goldwater's awkward alliance with racists launched a troubling trend. By elevating ideology over experience, the party of Lincoln was forging a strange new path. Those alliances, and the stubborn refusal to reexamine the choices that inspired them, continue to make the Republican Party a tough sell not just for African Americans, but for anyone outside the white community.

Why isn't libertarianism the solution to our post–Cold War political problems? Because a message of small government works only when it is tempered by a respect for the very real role that good government plays in guaranteeing freedom. A vigorous, ideological libertarianism is a recipe for privatized oppression.

Small government is a better prescription for personal liberty and economic success, but only if it remains strong enough to protect basic civil rights. It takes smart, nimble, effective government to guarantee a maximum range of personal choices. A government that is shrunk "down to the size where we can drown it in a bathtub" turns society into a playground for petty tyrants.

Moving Beyond Ideas

One crucial missing piece in contemporary American politics is a template of political policies relevant to our current needs. We are trapped in anachronistic political battles over the merits of one set of outdated ideas versus another. Pausing long enough to consider how the world has changed might give us room to find new, more relevant things to argue over.

Once we figure out how to fight over ideas that matter, how do we convert those ideas into policy? How do we re-engage the public in a way that can lead to effective political action?

A new, more relevant set of political ideas could refocus our attention on the problems that matter, but it still won't solve our most basic political deficit—our declining engagement. Having worked our way down the field, we still have that final, longest yard left to go. Building a smarter, more adaptable government can only be accomplished with a great deal more investment from ordinary people.

Part 4: Do Something

Leaving the office early tonight means extra work tomorrow, but it's the only way to get home in time for your son's soccer game. Your daughter's game starts half an hour later, so your spouse will be covering that one. After the game comes dinner, maybe around 7:30. You'll have to get it at the corner pizza joint—no time to cook.

Home by about 8, then baths, homework, clarinet practice, and so on. Once the kids are in bed, you've got a few emails to respond to, about matters that came up after you left the office.

Sitting in bed, spouses catch each other up on family matters. The kids' grades, weekend plans, news from work, the call from Grandma or Aunt so-and-so. Maybe you can squeeze in a half-hour episode from the DVR. Then the lights go out, and soon it's time to start all over again.

Where in this scenario is there room to attend a caucus?

Crazy politics is symptomatic of a complex social problem. Our system is built on the assumption that citizens are knitted together in a dense network of participatory institutions. Relatively few of those institutions are overtly political, but all of them foster an atmosphere of accountability and oversight that keeps our interests connected.

These networks maintain the feedback loops that dampen political stupidity. Very few people may be directly involved in politics in ways that require a physical presence, but that complex network of social institutions is supposed to ensure that those few people are sound, representative, and accountable. That isn't happening now.

As we've grown richer and freer, we've left behind many of the ties that once bound us together in communities. Greater individualism is fueling an expansion of wealth while tearing down many of the institutions that gave rise to that wealth.

In evaluating how we might restore some sanity to our political system, we must confront some bad news: For a representative democracy to thrive, there is no substitute for engagement. Time and attention come at a cost. The energy we devote to collective participation in community institutions must come from somewhere.

The good news is that we can leverage the same technological advancements that have sped up our lives in order to build new sorts of communities to supplement our personal engagement. Technology cannot replace the inherently humanizing value of face-to-face interactions. To the extent that we leverage its potential, we must always be aware of the fresh problems and distortions it creates. But, despite its limitations, we must start using these new tools more aggressively, and in a more purposeful manner, to re-create some of the institutional checks and balances that once rose from local communities.

Making these new virtual communities effective starts with an understanding of the older functions we need to supplement. Responsible citizenship involves so much more than reading the newspaper and voting. A complex political environment lurks beneath the headlines, as evidenced by the seemingly unimportant races hiding at the bottom of my Election Day ballot.

The Most Important Election of Our Lifetime

Next November we may be voting in the most important election of our lifetime, but which election is that?

Every four years, the bulk of our attention is devoted to the one race in which we each have the least influence. Meanwhile the really pivotal elections, the ones that sculpt our political landscape, tend to be hiding where we least expect them.

156

In 1996, a small-town city councilman ran for mayor on a novel strategy. Bypassing boring issues such as sales-tax collection and zoning, she ran on religion, abortion, and gun control. Flouting the legally nonpartisan character of the office, she won official backing from the state Republican Party. Out of that election, Wasilla, Alaska, got its "first Christian mayor," Sarah Palin.

In 1987, San Francisco's city supervisor, Harry Britt, had plans to take his popularity to Congress. Britt had solid backing in the city and needed only to defeat a party operative who had never held a public office. Britt narrowly lost his primary race to Nancy Pelosi. That fall she won her seat with fewer than 20,000 votes.

Alice Palmer promised in 1995 to step down from the Illinois State Senate in pursuit of an open congressional seat. When she lost the special election for Congress, she reneged on her promise and decided to run for reelection to the State Senate. At the last minute she submitted a slapdash nominating petition filled with mostly ineligible signatures. Her petition was invalidated, and she was kicked off the ballot. In 1996, her seat was won by a young law professor and community organizer named Barack Obama.

The presidential race is to American democracy what Easter Sunday is to churches. On the one hand, it's an opportunity to reach out and showcase the values and meaning of the institution to a group of people who may be only barely engaged. On the other hand, it's a chance to fill the building with uninvolved people who won't be there next week to contribute their time, energy, or money to keep the operation running.

The race for the presidency is so far removed from our day-to-day lives that we treat it like a game. Few things better symbolize the ways that the political-entertainment complex has distorted our involvement in the political system than the spectacle of presidential politics. More and more, voting for president is like watching *American Idol*, or submitting a Major League All-Star ballot.

Meanwhile, farther down the ballot are races that will determine what the president can and cannot do. Those races decide what happens to our local schools, whether we will commute to work each day on highways or trains, how much we'll pay in property or sales taxes.

Lurking there in the confusing thicket at the end of our ballots are races in which our votes count enormously. Somewhere north of 200 million people will cast a vote for president in 2016. But, for example, in Texas a potential state legislator might need only 25,000 votes to win.

This fall, perhaps a future president will be on your ballot for county commissioner or the state legislature. The choices we make in races all over the ballot, in elections happening all over the country, construct the pond in which our senior politicians swim. The more principled and rational that field of officials is, the better our system at large will function. The goofier they are—well, you know.

Down-ballot elections are a gateway to understanding how politics in our system actually plays out. Elections are important, but not as important as you might think. Our right to vote is an essential check on those who might abuse the public trust or compromise our basic freedoms, but voting is one of our least powerful avenues of political expression.

Have you ever looked at that list of names on the ballot and wondered who they are or how they got there? Have you ever wanted a broader range of choices? Those choices are available, but they require involvement much earlier in the process, long before any ballot is cast.

Perhaps it seems like the candidates on your general-election ballot do not represent your interests. Those candidates represent the interests of the people who placed them there through their active involvement. By the time I get to the voting booth, 95% of the work of politics has already been done. Voting is the method by which we ratify or veto someone else's work.

On Election Day, we are presented with a template of choices drawn up for us by people who have been shaping it for years, by organizing debates, talking with their neighbors, participating in community or business organizations, writing letters to candidates or to their local newspaper, volunteering on campaigns, donating money, or following hundreds of other avenues of influence.

If politics isn't about voting or winning elections, then what is it about? Politics in our system is driven by institutions, thousands of organizations of all types and sizes in which people aggregate their influence, sometimes for purposes that aren't explicitly political. Our candidates and ballot initiatives emerge from that network of institutions.

As I described in Part 2, those institutions are weaker and less effective than they used to be, with important consequences. Influencing politics in a serious way means participating in some form of interest group. A demonstration of the limited importance of elections, the power of operating through institutions, and the declining power of traditional institutions to maintain a healthy political environment can be seen with a look at the career of former Congressman Ron Paul.

Politics Is Not About Elections

By any conventional yardstick, Ron Paul is a failed politician. Sure, he served 12 terms in the House, but that achievement leaves him trailing such towering figures as Dante Fascell (19 terms), Ralph Regula (18 terms), and dozens of other long-serving congressmen you've never heard of. His legislative agenda was a complete failure. Every one of his numerous campaigns for higher office ended in defeat.

Ron Paul lost almost every major political battle he fought. And yet he has to be considered one of the most influential political figures of the past 20 years. Understanding how those two sentences can make sense together is to the key to recognizing how our politics works.

Paul did what John McCain, in the wake of his failed 2000 nominating campaign, declined to do—transform election losses into a wider political movement. Each of Paul's failed campaigns was a tool to refine his organization, gain new precinct chairs and convention delegates, and eat away at the old Reaganite policy establishment in the Republican Party issue by issue, plank by plank.

Despite his reputation for uncompromising politics, Paul carefully modified his brand over the years. He distanced himself from the hard-edged racism of his '80s-era mimeographed newsletters, though he has remained understandably popular among the extreme white-nationalist fringe. He tempered his stances to shape a modern neo-Confederate movement in which traditional libertarians and Southern religious fundamentalists can find room to collaborate. This emerging coalition between libertarians and social conservatives, best seen in the success of his son Rand, has formed the ideological core of the Tea Party movement.

John McCain, after his 2000 loss, played the game by its conventional rules, molding himself into the shape of a candidate who could win an election. Paul, by contrast, molded himself into a candidate who could shape public policy over a long time span. McCain was tied in knots by the demands of "winning" in 2008, badly limiting his ability to broaden his appeal. In the eight years after his loss to George W. Bush, he prepared a campaign infrastructure, but he declined a build a movement. To do so would have been too controversial, too much of a departure from the standard political script.

160

McCain declined to leverage the energy from his 2000 campaign to build his own institutional structures, convinced that by playing by the rules he could simply assume leadership over existing Republican institutions. McCain's loss in 2008, after years of carefully calculated insider posturing, has left him greatly diminished as a political force. Ron Paul, on the other hand, disregarded conventional definitions of victory and built a movement that is prepared to extend well beyond his own political career.

Paul's success matters because even though he failed to ever capture the Republican presidential nomination, the movement he built has constrained the policy options of the winners. Paul's followers were a force at the 2012 Republican National Convention, and they continue to influence practice and policy in state and local Republican organizations all over the country.

Coming in Ron Paul's wake is Rand Paul, a far more telegenic character who has mastered the neo-Confederate synergy of Antebellum Dixie economics and olde-tyme religion. The organization Ron Paul has built could reach a tipping point under Rand's influence.

Ron Paul's success should be particularly instructive for pragmatic, business-oriented Republicans bent on regaining some influence over their party. The short-term compromises required to win one particular election will accomplish nothing if, in the process, you surrender all of the power you might otherwise have been able to wield.

Politics is not about winning elections. Politics is about wielding power. Tuesday night's election results do not matter unless you have the influence and institutional weight on Wednesday morning to do something with your position.

What About Money?

It has become fashionable to assume that money is the only force in politics that really matters. There's an all-too-comfortable cynicism in the premise that some anonymous clutch of millionaires holed up in a swanky ski resort is pulling the strings that make our leaders dance. Belief in such an idea lets us off the hook for our own failures while relieving us of our sense of duty.

In reality, money is just a proxy for political involvement, a means of extending one's reach. Real power in representative politics comes from direct personal engagement on a mass, organized scale. Money is merely the next best thing, a substitute for organization that gains in relative value as our level of public engagement declines.

Wealthy individuals and corporations have relatively more influence over politics than you or I *individually* have. They always have, and perhaps they always will. The wealthy have more time, better access, and, typically, better education than the general public. What they lack is numbers.

Our political system is designed to vest power in numbers, spreading influence as broadly as possible. No one counts money on election night. Wealthy individuals still tend to exert more relative influence than poor individuals. Nonetheless, we should recognize that the relative power of the wealthy over our political system is in steady, long-term decline, and that's a big achievement.

Much of the superficial evidence for the power of money in politics rises from a strange paradox. Our new, somewhat awkward, and poorly shaped efforts to blunt wealthy donors' influence through regulation have led to unintended consequences. We have inadvertently raised the cost of running for office while simultaneously increasing the effort required to raise money. Misguided and malformed campaign-finance regulations have actually made fund-raising an obsession and handed additional leverage to donors.

We could take some simple, constitutionally valid steps that would further limit the relative power of monied interests, but those measures might run counter to our expectations of what effective campaign-finance reform looks like. As with many of the other recommendations in this piece, they hinge on the understanding that simpler is often better. They start with a better understanding of the progress we have already made.

Imagine a place in which only wealthy people can vote. The threshold for political influence at any level is a minimal amount of property ownership. Women are not allowed to participate at all, regardless of wealth. Only people of the correct race, family heritage, and religious associations are granted any voice.

Add in the legal protection of slaveholder's rights, and that is the system our Founders constructed. The American Republic was originally built to protect the liberty of wealthy white males. When you place the power of the wealthy in a historical context, the steady decline of their relative influence starts to become clearer.

America didn't grant voting rights to all white men until the 1820s. We didn't end slavery until the 1860s. Women didn't gain the right to vote until 1919. Blacks and Hispanics were routinely blocked from the political system until the 1970s and still have their influence systematically blunted today.

There were no federal campaign-finance laws of any kind until the Tillman Act in 1907. Until the early 20th century, Senate seats were more or less openly purchased with payments to the state legislators who selected Senators. That act required no disclosures and included no enforcement mechanism, accomplishing precisely nothing. There were no enforceable federal laws limiting campaign contributions until 1972. Ambassadorships to attractive, peaceful locations are still sold to the highest bidder, as they always have been.

State efforts to contain bribery and limit the ability to use wealth to tip the political scales are a patchwork of varying effectiveness. Some states have relatively clean elections. Some places, like Texas, have few rules, making it virtually impossible to prosecute anyone even for outright bribery. In general, it is not only legal but an established practice for corporations and the wealthy to use money to influence political outcomes at the state and local levels across much of the country.

There have only been two meaningful federal efforts to limit the influence of the wealthy on our politics. The first was a collection of Nixon-era legislation, and the second was McCain-Feingold in 2002. Both have been gutted by subsequent laws and the courts and today lie in ruins. Apart from bureaucratic restrictions promulgated and occasionally enforced by the Federal Election Commission, at the federal level we are more or less in the same place we were a century ago in terms of campaign-finance laws.

There are few explicit, enforceable legal checks on the political influence of money. Yet buying a political outcome in our system is harder now than it has ever been. It costs more; it requires more effort, energy, and coordination; and more attempts fail than succeed. The decline in the relative power of money in our politics is almost entirely a product of the large devolutionary trends outlined earlier, rather than the result of any legislative effort.

True, well-funded special interests are still more powerful than they should be. Reducing the disproportionate influence of money on our politics should be a priority. However, money is not our central political problem. Finding an intelligent way forward starts with a realistic assessment of the situation.

The most powerful force in our politics is the time, energy, and attention of people willing to get off their couch and participate personally in the process. It takes enormous sums of money to counter the influence of a few well-organized and connected activists.

History is littered with failed self-funded campaigns by millionaire political tourists. For every Bloomberg or Rauner, there are dozens of Fiorinas and Forbeses. Yes, a rich person has a wider opportunity to personally and independently influence political outcomes than I do, but that opportunity is not nearly as wide as most people assume.

When does money carry the most influence? Money has highly disproportionate influence when it is coordinated with a popular movement and combined with a focused lobbying campaign in Washington. That isn't easy. It requires far more than just writing a check and walking away.

Perhaps the most famous modern example of successful political spending is the tightly coordinated campaigns of the Koch brothers. They aren't merely flinging checks. Across decades of concentrated effort, they have built networks of grassroots activists integrated with Washington think tanks and lobbying efforts. One of their projects, a PAC called FreedomWorks, facilitated years of grassroots-organizing forums that eventually gave birth to the Tea Party movement.

Through coordinated action with a dedicated core of allied institutions and volunteers, the Koch brothers are able to steer the political system toward otherwise unpopular positions. Yes, they are rich, and yes, that money has played a vital role in their political success, but their success came from building a strategic linkage between community activists and their Washington lobbying efforts.

That said, the way to gauge the influence of money in politics is the return on investment. It isn't easy to measure exactly how much the Koch brothers' effort has cost, but their affiliated groups plan to raise and spend approximately $800 million in the 2016 election cycle. Spread that kind of spending out on an upward-slanting arc across the two decades of the brothers' efforts—that looks like a lot of money pouring into politics. It is, but don't miss the point: *That's how much money it takes to fight against the tide created by individuals' simple political engagement.*

As for what has that money has accomplished for the Kochs: It has certainly given them unique access to political figures, but concrete political successes are hard to identify. Their highest-profile objectives, repealing the Affordable Care Act and gaining approval for the Keystone Pipeline, have failed decisively.

They have *probably* been instrumental in preventing a handful of states from embracing Medicaid expansion, and in limiting union power in Wisconsin and Michigan. Apart from those examples, it is very difficult to find other initiatives they managed to push into policy that otherwise lacked public support. They have been reasonably successful mostly in stalling policy rather than making it.

That limited scope of achievement still makes them the most successful buyers of political outcomes in America. When those accomplishments are measured against the hundreds of millions of dollars and endless hours of coordination they required, the challenge of buying political outcomes becomes clear.

When does money fail to yield political influence? Money is almost useless when spent on campaign contributions without any institutional network to support the effort. Billionaire political oddball Sheldon Adelson was able to personally fund an entire campaign for the Republican nomination in 2012 with tens of millions in personal investment. Without his support, Newt Gingrich would probably not have been able to compete.

And for his money, Adelson got nearly nothing. His candidate lost, and his causes, whatever they are, still are waiting for a champion. True, Adelson has more access to powerful people than most of us do, but as a fabulously wealthy person with an elite network he would have had that without writing a single check.

The simple fact of the matter is that a vast majority of the arm's-length campaign contributions coming from wealthy individuals or anyone else are motivated by support for something a candidate is already promoting. They don't buy much, if anything. A guy who donated $1 million to a political party or campaign can get access to senior officials that you cannot, but that doesn't mean he can buy a policy outcome.

More important, the guy who can afford to make a $1 million campaign contribution was probably already in a position to get that access. That's what we need to understand when we evaluate the influence of the rich on politics and how to contain it.

If it seems like public officials are spending more time and energy than ever raising money, that's because they are. By a strange twist, our weak campaign-finance laws are to blame for this situation. Our complicated, confusing, and often contradictory mess of regulations has made it extremely difficult to run for office. It has also provided a surprising advantage for wealthy donors.

Thirty years ago, a candidate could fund a campaign with an appeal to one or two donors. As a result, he might be very closely aligned with that one interest, but he spent very little time soliciting money. Now a candidate still needs wealthy donors, but she has to find dozens or even hundreds of them in order to survive. Instead of forging an appeal to a few donors with whom she is already aligned on policy, the candidate must build an agenda that will appeal to wealthy donors *as a class*. Our funding limits have acted like a union for the wealthy, allowing them to act together in ways that would have been impossible without those limits.

At the same time, the pressure to find donors has increased the power of third-party interest groups and PACs that seek to influence campaigns without being specifically tied to a candidate. A Congressional candidate has only so many hours of the day to spend raising money. These organizations have gained unnecessary influence as caps on campaign contributions have raised the pressure to find cash. They are also competing with candidates for funds.

In short, our approach to campaign-finance law has been an unmitigated disaster. Building a more intelligent system starts with a closer look at the behavior we hope to limit. We want our elected officials to make policy decisions based on a combination of their constituents' input and their own well-considered evaluations of the public and national interest. Limits on campaign contributions are meant to halt the wealthy from engaging in a sort of legalized bribery that would subvert the public interest in favor of their own.

Not every campaign contribution is bribery. Campaign contributions are in fact one of the ways that we measure a potential candidate's credibility and qualifications. It takes money to run for office. Communicating with voters costs money. Driving from campaign site to campaign site costs money. Taking money out of politics would require us to take most of the communication, visibility, and accountability out of politics.

Perhaps the simplest, most effective means to limit the power of organized bribery to subvert the public interest is to build our campaign-finance system on bedrock of full disclosure. Instead of limiting contributions by amount, we should impose authentic transparency.

No one should be allowed to make an anonymous political donation. No money spent on a political campaign should be collected so close to an election date that full public disclosure is impossible. Every contribution should be traceable to a living, breathing human being who will be accountable for their actions.

Thanks to the Supreme Court's decision in *Citizens United*, implementing some of these provisions might be complicated, but it would not be impossible. The disclosure requirements might not prevent corporations from making donations, but the requirements could be written to require the disclosure to provide contact information for every board member and executive, at least helping to stem the tide of dark money flowing from sham organizations.

With or without a better approach to campaign finance, it is vital that the public not lose sight of the bigger picture. Our involvement is key.

The 2012 presidential campaign cost a staggering $2 billion in direct spending on both sides. It's a big number, but like a lot of other big numbers it's pretty meaningless by itself. The massive, nationwide marketing campaign that leads to the White House costs less than Americans spend on Halloween candy every year. We spend $350 million a year on pet costumes. Scale matters.

The average cost to run a successful campaign for the Senate has actually declined in inflation-adjusted terms since the '80s. The cost to run a House campaign as increased, though this probably reflects the higher levels of competition in Congressional campaigns since the relatively stagnant period in the mid-20th century.

The best way to limit the power of a few wealthy campaign contributors right now is to get off the couch and get involved in public institutions, in even the simplest form. Money is powerful, but we can blunt its influence with a very modest effort.

Five local chapters of a mothers' group with 20 active members each may be able to counter the influence of a well-crafted $250,000 political spend. But when the involvement and participation in those groups falls below a critical mass, that $250,000 contribution, or the deceptive radio campaign it funded, may be the only coherent voice a candidate hears on a very specific issue. Our apathy is a gift to those who want to buy political outcomes.

Say what you will about campaign finance, lobbyists, and the rich. When you look closely at the matter, one stark fact becomes clear: The government we have is the government we earned. To get better government we'll have to become better citizens.

Joining a Political Party

The most direct and obvious way to get involved in politics is to volunteer locally with a political party. Across much the country, the simplest way to do this is to offer to serve as the head of a precinct.

What this job is called (committeeman, chairman, captain, etc.), the influence it wields, and how it operates varies a great deal depending on where you live and which party you join. What is nearly universal is the need inside both major parties for more of them.

Generally, a precinct chair is the party's liaison to a local community. The size of a precinct is usually no more than a few blocks. In a major city, that might be 100–200 households in a walkable circuit. It is generally meant to be a unit that one person can canvass in a couple of weekends.

Depending on the jurisdiction, precinct chairs may be responsible for voter registration, finding election judges, and participating in decisions for a county or town party organization. The most crucial element of the job is voter turnout, making sure a party's most committed voters know about and participate in elections. A precinct chair is a community organizer.

Rarely does the job involve any financial commitment. The time commitment varies and is generally flexible based on what you can offer. Doing the job well during election season will seldom require fewer than a couple of hours a week and may also require some time during work hours on election day. In some jurisdictions, the precinct chair is expected to organize a precinct meeting in connection with primaries or caucuses.

Some locales have opportunities to serve in a sort of gap-filling capacity by assisting a precinct chair. This requires less time, and in many cases you will be supervised by a long-tenured chairman. Such an approach offers a chance to learn the ropes and gauge whether you're ready for a more involved role. With levels of public participation in just about every form of social capital declining, political parties are short on volunteers everywhere. If you are interested in participating, they will generally find a way to put you to work.

Keep in mind that direct participation with a party might not be your ideal method for getting involved. Depending on where you live, these organizations are often filled with the truest of true believers. If you're not exactly sure where you fit on the political spectrum or how involved you want to be, you might experience some discomfort in this crowd.

That said, people committed to public service but uncomfortable with strident partisanship are positioned to play a vital role inside our political parties if they have the stomach to stay involved. They may be the key to the parties' survival and continued effectiveness. If you can stand it, participation in your local political party may offer the most value you can wring from whatever time you are willing to invest in public involvement.

Fortunately, for those who are put off by partisan politics, myriad other opportunities are available to shape our political landscape in less direct ways.

Small Groups, Big Influence

The Houston Realty Business Coalition hosts monthly breakfast meetings featuring some of the most influential figures in state and local politics. Founded in 1967, the HRBC (which used to stand for the Houston Realty Breakfast Club) is an institutional hub for Houston's business conservatives.

Breakfast with the HRBC offers an opportunity to hear, meet, or button-hole ambitious political figures at every stage of their career. If you are considering a run for office in the Houston area, particularly on the Republican ballot, the HRBC is a room you will probably have to work successfully in order to win. If you have a political issue you want to bring to the attention of someone in charge, or someone who might one day be in charge, a table at the HRBC is an excellent place to get yourself heard.

Speakers invited to address a meeting get a valuable free forum to promote their campaign or explain a policy agenda. The real action, though, is around the tables. Breakfast at the HRBC is a chance to meet tomorrow's congressional candidates as they campaign now for a job on the courts or school board, for a county-executive office, or for another local role. The invited speaker may be a political figure who has already achieved prominence, but all around the table are future candidates and the influencers who will steer them. It is an opportunity to learn something about these candidates on a personal level before placing them in a position to impact your life.

What makes the HRBC and groups like it particularly powerful is their multifunctional nature. The HRBC is not a political party. It is closely tied to the GOP, but many meetings feature Democratic speakers and guests. Activism is its primary function. It is officially registered as a PAC and makes open political endorsements. The real power of the group, though, is its deep roots that extend beyond politics.

HRBC is also a business club. The members and leadership may share core political ideas, but they must also work together in the real-estate community on a day-to-day basis. Wielding influence inside the HRBC requires more than paying a fee, showing up, and spouting an opinion. Relationships formed outside the meetings and beyond the scope of politics can increase or decrease one's political sway at the breakfast table. These people encounter one another in business and social life. Pig-headed political incivility at breakfast can impact one's bottom line in business.

In short, this overlap between politics and extra-political interests helps to keep a lid on the most-extreme impulses of the group's individual members. There is only so much irrational, uncivil behavior one can afford to indulge before it begins to create pressure on one's day job. The members maintain a complex accountability to one another that inspires at least some modicum of moderation.

Organizations like the HRBC have a clear financial dimension to them. It costs money to attend, roughly $50 a month on a per-meeting basis or an annual fee of $350. Access to the breakfast table, though certainly not affordable for everyone, is relatively open. That's true of most similar organizations across the spectrum—the membership fee is low enough to be broadly accessible while high enough to weed out the tourists.

Groups like the HRBC are built on personal networks. Nothing stops the random yahoo off the street from laying down $50 and showing up, but that doesn't happen a lot. Very few people outside of real estate or Houston politics even know about it. The organization does not advertise or actively promote itself. Most members first learned about it through an invitation from a friend or colleague.

For Houston residents who can spare a few early-morning hours once a month and can absorb the modest cost, the HRBC offers a chance to participate in their government in a uniquely powerful way. Similar opportunities exist all over the spectrum, from partisan political organizations to PTAs, service clubs, and business groups.

Our political system is not built on elections. It is not built on money. It is built on the hundreds of thousands of institutions, like the Houston Realty Business Coalition, that tie us together in bonds of common interest and accountability. These institutions are where the real work of politics gets done. Political influence rises from the careful, strategic investment of time and effort in these organizations.

The health of those institutions determines how much influence can be purchased at what price. It also determines how much is really at stake on election day.

The PTA Path to Power

Thom Tillis, formerly a state representative and the speaker of the North Carolina House of Representatives, is now a Republican U.S. senator. He has a long history of public service stretching back to his years on his local town board and even a stint as a PTA president. He was elected to the North Carolina General Assembly in 2006. He became speaker of the state House in 2011 and was elected to the Senate in 2014.

By contrast, former Representative Paul Broun, from Georgia, started his career in public service by running unsuccessfully for Congress in 1990. He lost three attempts at federal office before squeaking out a victory in a low-turnout special election in 2007. Broun vied for a U.S. Senate seat in 2014, declining to run for re-election again in order to do so. He lost in the primary.

Broun and Tillis are both deeply religious. They are both very conservative Republicans from Southern states. It would be difficult to find any policy positions of importance on which they disagree in a material way. Yet the two men, as public figures, could not be more different.

Tillis is a level-headed pragmatist with a record of tangible achievements in government. He's a solid leader who seldom makes a gaffe. Broun is a walking, talking cartoon character who can claim no political accomplishments beyond his own election victories. Broun consistently makes bizarre and occasionally disturbing comments that provide ammunition for opponents without doing anything to advance a credible legislative agenda.

The two are contemporaries, but Tillis has taken the traditional route to political power, working his way up through the community from one position of trust to the next. Along the way, Tillis has been vetted and proven, building ties of accountability that influence and constrain his actions.

Broun represents the emerging avenue to political influence based on money, extremism, ambition and persistence. Broun has been banging on the doors of power for 25 years without establishing the kind of ties that impose discipline or accountability. Broun is the "outsider," representing a political trend away from community accountability in favor of outlandish, crowd-pleasing antics.

Broun has passed uncomfortably through the body politic, contributing little more than a montage of embarrassing sound bites. Tillis is a senator and likely to remain an influential figure for many years thanks to the depth of the ties he has built over time. Yet these men might not have been so different as public figures but for the paths they took to power. Perhaps the key difference between the two men can be found in that stint at the PTA.

Choosing to launch a career of public service by first serving the community in which you live is a decision with consequences. It means that the base of power you construct will be filled with people who know your kids, people who know where you live. The community imposes constraints and discipline.

It means that one of the first political lessons you learn is how to mediate passionate differences among people who share common interests. Ideological commitment is of little use at a town-hall, school-board, or PTA meeting. These institutions are judged by concrete accomplishments, by problems solved.

Inflammatory rhetoric will get you nowhere at the PTA. A career that grows out of this environment is likely to be much more responsible, accountable, and effective than that of a millionaire dilettante entering politics as a tourist. For those who would like to serve in political offices of high profile and power, perhaps the best place to start is on their own block.

Small-scale local institutions like PTAs, service organizations, even kids' sports clubs build the social connections that support healthy politics. Even for people with no interest in political issues, these groups form a platform that let them influence the process in the most subtle and indirect, yet powerful, ways. Involvement in local clubs and organizations may be more important and powerful than voting.

Should I Vote?

In Texas's 2010 Republican primary, an appointed incumbent to the powerful state Railroad Commission faced re-election. He was qualified and had a long record of related service. He had a $600,000 campaign budget—massive for the office he was seeking—and enjoyed the full backing of his party with no organized opposition.

That appointed incumbent lost his primary by a wide margin to a random guy who signed up to run, did not campaign, and raised less than $40,000 for the race. What issue or scandal doomed the commissioner's campaign? There wasn't one. How dissatisfied were voters with his performance? Not at all. Why did he lose? The incumbent's name is Victor Carrillo. The name of his virtually unknown opponent is David Porter. Victor Carrillo lost his primary to a random Anglo surname.

A primary is low-turnout election. The Texas Railroad Commission is a body few people know or care anything about. While the Commission is powerful and important, its duties are technical. Requirements to effectively perform the job have precious little to do with partisan ideology. This is precisely the kind of race in which ballot order, name recognition, or something as simple as an ethnic identity play an outsize role in the results. In other words, this is the kind of race in which we should all seriously consider not voting.

Our right to vote is the central guarantor of our freedom, the threshold characteristic of authentic citizenship. Without it we are subject to the will of others. Our commitment to participate in elections is the foundation of responsible citizenship.

If voting is truly powerful, than like any other power it is vulnerable to abuse. Ideally, prior to any election, I will do some research on the races. I will seek out the opinions of people I trust. I will find out which candidates are prepared for office and which ones are political tourists. I will select candidates in the same manner and with the same rigor with which I select a doctor or an accountant or a day-care center.

On the one hand, down-ballot races are far more important than most people realize and deserve more attention than they currently get. On the other hand, if we lack the time or interest to learn about those races, we should back away from influencing their outcomes.

Low-information voting is a lot like shooting in the dark: It tends to do more harm than good. This should go without saying, but apparently it needs to be said. It is vital that we all participate in the political process, but *voting* and *participating* are not the same thing. If the only attention I'm going to devote to those races is to cast a blind vote, then perhaps I should give those races no attention at all.

Social Media and Social Capital

Political outcomes flow from political engagement. Voting is great. Staying current on the news is valuable. Contributing to campaigns helps. But there is no substitute for our direct personal involvement in public life, the so-called "social capital" on which our representative government is founded. Where does that mean for those tired working parents at the end of a grueling day? What opportunities can there be for a single mother or a stressed-out college student? Our faster, more prosperous lives leave little time for political engagement.

The same accelerating technological progress that has spawned our social-capital deficit is presenting us with previously unthinkable channels for engagement. Smart, deliberate efforts to build social organizations online might allow us to create new venues for public life and help busy, responsible citizens regain some of the political influence they have lost in the Information Age.

Social media can just as easily be part of the problem as a part of the solution. Social media by design is the opposite of social capital; it can easily be used to spread disinformation, fear, and extremism. As a platform, it eliminates locality and accountability: Online, I can assume any identity I want and engage with other people around the globe in ways that are very difficult to trace back to me. But these are the two primary characteristics of our old social-capital institutions that we must find ways to replicate in social media if it is going to prove helpful in restoring sanity to our politics.

Locality for a social-media network is important because it allows the group to wield a level of influence that can be readily converted into policy. Thirty well-organized people collaborating online can have a remarkable impact on a city-council or school-board election. By doing so, they establish themselves as attractive mediators for figures looking to organize at larger levels.

Having a geographic focus also keeps the group centered on issues with very concrete causes and effects. Dumb ideas about my local roads, schools, or law enforcement bring negative feedback in a relatively tight loop. Building on a small core geography breeds an interest in pragmatism that can impact the group's activism further up the political chain.

Finally, a geographic focus also fosters the other vital political interest normally eroded by social media: accountability. The anonymity of social networks creates a nearly irresistible drive toward extreme and irresponsible interactions. In a typical social-media setting, wild hyperbole and insults can often create a following while stifling any constructive exchange of ideas. When commenters know they will see one another at the train station or their kids' soccer games, much more thought and care is invested in protecting the forum itself.

That restraint has a valuable side benefit. The effort to keep matters civil also presses participants to hear one another. Social-media interactions that preserve a sense of accountability push their members toward understanding in order to find avenues of civil disagreement and dispute resolution.

Building local networks based on social media can run into some interesting challenges. Some of the conversations and interactions that we naturally understood in a personal or small-group setting do not work the same way in social media.

Over the course of breakfast at the Lions' Club, I might have a conversation about politics. The shape and tenor of that conversation might be tempered by what I know about the other eight or 10 people around the table. That conversation might be different in subtle but significant ways if I was sitting at the next table over, with a different mix of my neighbors.

My ability to communicate in such a nuanced manner based on the demands of a particular audience disappears when I send a message to the entire club's email-distribution list. Content that might have been appropriate and well received at a certain table might be inflammatory when sent to the whole group. In effect, social-media communication in many cases follows the same rules as giving a public speech, though the forum itself creates a misleading sense of intimacy.

Some of this disconnect is a function of the veneer of unanimity created by the ways we used to communicate in traditional social-capital networks. Politics, like religion, has long been regarded as an impolite subject for light conversation. The absence of overt political discussion tended to subsume political disagreements, creating a false impression of consensus. We generally assumed that the range of political opinions among friends and neighbors was tighter than it actually was. The filtering effects of our social-capital networks reinforced that impression.

Social media has pulled back some of that veneer off political questions. The breadth of political disagreements, finally aired, can be jarring yet powerful. When social media is successfully combined with social capital, it may be possible to forge more authentic, enduring consensus based on an awareness of our differences as well as our common interests.

Building new networks of political accountability in a virtual space will compromise some of the values of our old institutions, but it may bring some new benefits we had not anticipated. The lower threshold of investment of time and money may serve to broaden participation, making our institutions more genuinely representative.

When we talk about making our system more accountable, we often refer to its effects on some abstract collection of poor or downtrodden citizens. In fact, the swath of our culture likely to benefit most from the political impact of social-media organizing is middle earners, early in their careers, with families and jobs.

Our traditional, social-capital-driven political culture offered outsize influence to people over 50, and especially those over 60. It is no accident that Americans over 55 live in what amounts to a European social-welfare state while everyone else enjoys the glories of virtually unfettered capitalism. Even in a slower age, they were the only block of people with the time available to meet the full demands of in-person politics.

Educated, professional, well-informed 30-somethings have traditionally enjoyed a tiny fraction of the political influence wielded by Americans over 60. They lack the time necessary to build well-organized interest groups. They lack experience in building social connections. Many of them are very mobile, still building careers and not yet settled into a familiar place. And the demands of family life stifle efforts to participate in-person in the kinds of networks that were once the only outlet for real political influence.

Yes, the poor may benefit from social media's loosening of the old political structure. The first noticeable impact, though, is likely to be an increase in the political influence and improvement in the living conditions of relatively successful but previously unrepresented young Americans.

As we begin to recognize the potential of social networks to re-create local, accountable ties, those networks can become the building blocks of a new power base that could stabilize a political system mired in dysfunction and extremism. But how? On a whiteboard, this picture looks promising, but making it real will be a challenge. What will these new, local, accountable networks look like? How will they operate? Who will build them? Who will participate?

What social-media social capital might look like

It is tough to provide examples of promising social-media approaches because platforms change so quickly. A helpful list at the time this is written could look hopelessly dated in a year. Yet some of the oldest, most staid, least interesting social-networking technologies, such as email distribution lists and online discussion forums, remain some of the most potent.

Neighborhood or street-block email distribution lists are simple and common. If you don't have a neighborhood or block email list, starting one can be a straightforward process. Such lists do not work well if they become explicitly political, but they can be a launch point for politically oriented organizing, by allowing people to identify like-minded neighbors for other lists or groups.

Meanwhile, newer technologies such as Reddit, Facebook, and Google+ enable you to organize activism from your living room. These platforms lack many of the finest characteristics of in-person social capital, but they also deliver some advantages. They are fast, they can incorporate many different information sources, and they make it easy for our local, accountable organizations to link up with other groups on the largest possible scale. They are more democratic, responsive, open, and cheaper to establish and maintain than older institutions.

When organizing toward a goal on social media, it is helpful to think of online networks as a pyramid. At the base are many networks, like neighborhood email lists, which are locally focused and relatively nonpartisan. At this level, politics is a relatively rare subject of interaction. What political content is shared is almost entirely nonpartisan and centered on matters related to school boards, city councils, or other neighborhood political action.

Out of these hyper-local interactions emerge additional email lists, or Reddit groups, or other forums, that take a more partisan tack on issues that are still largely local. A neighborhood or block email list covering 50-80 households might feed several more-focused lists, each of which might have 5-8 households from the larger list participating with 200-300 others from the town.

These aggregations might feed into and overlap with local political-party networks, or networks formed to work on specific issues. Contacts formed from a simple neighborhood distribution list might serve, with modest time and effort, as an opening to networks that extend nationally. Participation at multiple levels extends reach while retaining some the much-needed accountability that helps moderate our interactions.

What can overlapping networks like this accomplish? Everything from candidate recruitment to voter turnout to issue advocacy. Social-media social capital may not replicate all of the benefits of older social-capital institutions, but with an awareness of the opportunity and a bit of commitment, we may be able to build something even better. It all starts with a few keystrokes. It requires virtually no money and very little technical savvy. What it demands most is commitment.

A Better America for Two Hours a Month

After a long day at work followed by kids' band recitals, soccer games and other activities, a couple sits down to regroup before bed. Earlier that day they received an email from a friend planning to run for the school board.

A brief calendar check reveals an opening in two weeks and they send a reply to their friend offering to host a coffee for her in their home. A message to the neighborhood email list announces the 45-minute evening meeting. By morning, there are eight acceptances, and many who received the message are including other friends. On the evening of the event, 20 neighbors assemble to hear from the grateful candidate. The cost of the whole process comes down to the price of the coffee and snacks. Setting it up required no more than a few minutes of each person's time.

Just 20 years ago, organizing an event like that might have required hours of phone calls at a minimum, perhaps augmented by walking the block to knock on some doors. Social media makes it possible to do more with less, not only at work but in our public lives. One such effort builds on another, providing opportunities to influence the political process further up the chain.

A slice of time invested in helping a local candidate can quickly translate into opportunities to influence races farther up the ballot. Three people who organized coffee meetings for a city-council candidate could organize a brief meeting that would attract a congressional candidate. Those meetings translate into lingering influence that can still be wielded by keystrokes at the end of a day.

We don't have a lot of time, but a modest investment of interest and effort could be the force that restores some sanity to a political process gone mad. Technology and wealth may have destroyed our traditional social-capital infrastructure, but they have opened up exciting opportunities to build networks that could function better than past ones have.

Perhaps the initial goal of these efforts is political, but rebuilding social capital on a platform of social media might have some additional value. Social capital was never primarily about politics. Whether built around a service organization, or the PTA, or a church group, or a fraternal society, the main thrust of those physical networks was social. What made them function was a communal goal that kept people focused and engaged. Their value, however, was largely personal. These layers of social interaction helped keep us healthy and sane.

Bringing purpose, importance, and accountability to our otherwise pixel-deep social-media interactions may have some value for the culture at large. Social media has granted us an increased quantity of interactions, but they are largely missing quality. Introducing a shared sense of purpose and duty to our online communities might help to mitigate their empty-calorie effect.

America is still ours. More than perhaps ever before, we have the government we deserve. The same forces that have sped up, enriched, and liberated our lives have laid new political tools at our feet. Until we master those tools, our government will continue to get weirder, and the consequences of our disengagement will creep nearer and nearer to every door.

Two hours a month. Start there: two hours invested, at the most local level, in building relationships, knowing who your neighbors are, and shaping a social network. That's enough to transform a political structure gone mad into a political structure that reflects our best and highest values. If each of us would commit to such a modest investment of our most precious resource, we could regain control of our political system and change our future for the better.

Conclusion: The Optimists Are Winning

We are nearly always focused on what's wrong with the world. Our problems, not our achievements, demand our immediate attention. An extended description of the trouble in American politics and the difficulties we face can leave us with a distorted picture.

Our most daunting challenges have emerged as a consequence of triumphs more comprehensive and powerful than our ancestors dared imagine. We are fortunate in our problems.

The last globally relevant alternative to liberal democracy and market economics has collapsed. America stands alone as the world's only economic, political and military superpower. That victory has spawned new complexities we did not anticipate and still struggle to recognize, but those challenges are a gift.

Capitalism, absent proper constraint, commoditizes everything. Reckless market forces, growing wealth, and expanding personal freedom are undermining social capital and weakening the ties on which communities are built. Globalized markets bring spectacular complexity, making an older style of top-down bureaucratic government far too cumbersome to be effective. These trends are in turn putting dangerous stresses on our government.

In short, just like previous generations, we face the demand to adapt. Others have done it in the past, and we will now. Sometimes it pays to step back and look at what's working: Things do get better. Taking time to appreciate the progress we have made helps us maintain focus and hope. For human beings, the past 25 years have been marked by some stunning victories.

Globally, the number of people living in extreme poverty has dropped by half in only a generation. Out of the collapse of communism has emerged a massive global middle class. By 2030, almost two-thirds of the world's population will have moved into the global middle-income brackets.

For all the conflict and instability we see, there is not a single active war between nation-states on the planet. The age of American global military dominance has marked a historic low in military violence. The world is more peaceful than it has ever been.

Population growth has stabilized everywhere in the developed world, including China. Population-growth rates are in steep decline globally. Depending on events in Africa, we may be on track to see global population begin to decline in absolute numbers in less than 40 years.

In the U.S., most aspects of life have been improving at rates no one could have anticipated in 1990. Teen pregnancy, abortion, cocaine use, murder, crime, homelessness, and divorce are all in steep, long-term decline, a fact that has gone largely unnoticed.

The cost of almost everything is falling dramatically, with one very important and very positive exception. Human expertise is more valuable than it has ever been. Not only is the number of Americans getting a college education climbing, that climb is accelerating. Why does college cost so much? One reason might be the good news just listed. Another might be the next bit of good news.

High-school graduation rates are the highest they have ever been in the U.S., and heading toward 90%. For all the hand-wringing about U.S. schools, we are educating more of our people than ever by a very wide margin.

When technology, health-care improvements, crime, and the declining cost of nearly everything is taken into account, even America's least fortunate are radically richer, freer, and safer than they were just a generation ago.

One of the hottest neighborhoods in New York City is Harlem. Brooklyn is trendy.
Twenty years ago Dr. Dre was producing a particularly angry brand of rap music; now he is a billionaire tech entrepreneur. Michael Jordan, Magic Johnson, 50 Cent, and a very long list of other, mostly obscure former "stars" have made more money in business than they did in their entertainment careers. African-Americans from all kinds of backgrounds are making the transition from "rich" to "wealthy."

The Chicago River, which not so long ago was a sewer, now hosts kayak tours through the city's downtown. Since the passage of the Nixon-era environmental-protection acts, our nation's air and water have become remarkably clean, even in the middle of big cities.

Thanks to a boom in energy production in the U.S., Mexico, and Canada, America is now effectively energy independent. We may be capable of meeting all of our energy demand from sources within our own borders within 20 years. Our natural-gas imports alone have fallen by almost 70% in less than a decade.

And green energy is no longer a dream. Dark, rainy Germany is on track to generate a third of its power from solar energy alone by 2020. The price of solar energy has dropped by half in just five years. In sunny parts of Asia, solar power is already cheaper than gas. It is expected to be cheaper than fossil fuels globally within five years.

The most exciting new sports car in America is powered by electricity. It isn't built in Detroit or Mexico or Brazil, but in suburban San Francisco.

The U.S. is the only global military power on the planet. Russia still maintains one aircraft carrier. It has to be accompanied on missions by a fleet of tugboats. No other military force, apart from our European allies, is even close to being able to operate beyond their borders. We possess the only offense-capable "defensive" force on Earth.

The United States is also the wealthiest nation on the planet, and the margin isn't close. Our economy produced just short of $16 trillion in 2013. The second-ranked country, China, came in at less than $10 trillion, but that number appears to be radically distorted. China's population is more than four times as large as the U.S. Its GDP per capita ranks 83rd, roughly the same as Peru's.

But aren't we bankrupt? Hardly. Our debt is growing, but that was not always the case and need not be. Just over a decade ago we were debating what to do with a massive projected surplus. George W. Bush took office with a budget plan, inherited from his predecessor, that was projected to pay off the national debt entirely by 2009. Eight years later, Obama inherited a budget that created the largest single-year deficit in American history.

We could get back in the black with a modest tax increase, a few changes in defense and safety-net spending, and a fraction of a point increase in economic growth. We've had a formal, bipartisan plan on the table to do this since 2010. We haven't done it because the people who claim to care the most about our debt seem to care more about other priorities.

Our debt is having zero economic impact in the present and will have no impact on the economy in the foreseeable future. It is purely a political problem.

We live in an extraordinary time of peace, freedom, and wealth, and we are almost entirely blind to it. Conditions for Americans and the rest of the world could be, and probably will be, even better in the future. How much better things will get, and for how many people, will depend to a very large extent on decisions that Americans make in coming years. Moving beyond the politics of crazy could open up access to a better world, not just a better country.

Progress means graduating up to better and better problems. We will cope with those new problems more capably if we properly appreciate our accomplishments. We are winning. Step by step we are doing what our ancestors have done for centuries and millennia, evolving to meet new challenges in our environment by adapting our culture and technology. With commitment and a little work, we will do it again, and again, and again...

About the Author

Chris Ladd is a Texan living in the Chicago area. He has been active in grassroots Republican politics for most of his life, first in Texas and now as a precinct committeeman in the Chicago suburbs.

He has been blogging at the Houston Chronicle since 2008 and maintains a blog of his own at GOPLifer.com. His work has appeared on David Frum's FrumForum, the Huffington Post, Washington Times, the Chicago Tribune's ChicagoNow blogs, and other outlets. *The Politics of Crazy* is his first book.

Chris earned a BA in Political Science from Southwestern University in Georgetown, Texas and a JD from the University of Houston. He has a wife and two children and a career in the software industry.

46642030R00107

Made in the USA
San Bernardino, CA
11 March 2017